T0129698

It's *Not* about Me

A Guide to an Amazing Marriage

—— KEN HINKLEY ——

WESTBOW
PRESS®
A DIVISION OF THOMAS NELSON
& ZONDERVAN

This book is a work of non-fiction. Unless otherwise noted, the author and the publisher make no explicit guarantees as to the accuracy of the information contained in this book and in some cases, names of people and places have been altered to protect their privacy.

WestBow Press books may be ordered through booksellers or by contacting:

WestBow Press
A Division of Thomas Nelson & Zondervan
1663 Liberty Drive
Bloomington, IN 47403
www.westbowpress.com
1 (866) 928-1240

Because of the dynamic nature of the Internet, any web addresses or links contained in this book may have changed since publication and may no longer be valid. The views expressed in this work are solely those of the author and do not necessarily reflect the views of the publisher, and the publisher hereby disclaims any responsibility for them.

Any people depicted in stock imagery provided by Getty Images are models, and such images are being used for illustrative purposes only. Certain stock imagery © Getty Images.

Scriptures taken from the Holy Bible, New International Version®, NIV®. Copyright © 1973, 1978, 1984, 2011 by Biblica, Inc.™ Used by permission of Zondervan. All rights reserved worldwide. www.zondervan.com The "NIV" and "New International Version" are trademarks registered in the United States Patent and Trademark Office by Biblica, Inc.™

ISBN: 978-1-9736-8788-7 (sc)
ISBN: 978-1-9736-8789-4 (hc)
ISBN: 978-1-9736-8787-0 (e)

Library of Congress Control Number: 2020904461

Print information available on the last page.

WestBow Press rev. date: 03/11/2020

Contents

Before You Wed: Personal Decisions
You Must Make

Coming Together as One

After You're Wed: Facing Life's
Challenges Together

Appendix

Acknowledgments

I must give credit for this book to many people. First of all to my wife, who has guided me for more than forty years. She truly remains my helpmeet. I want to thank all the members of the Rumford writers group, whose contribution is beyond measure. And most of all, I want to thank my Lord, who has opened my eyes to many truths through his word and his working in my life and the lives of others.

Although this work describes real-life incidences, all names are either changed or are fictitious to protect the identities of those involved.

Introduction

Marriage is not about you. Nearly everyone enters a relationship, on whatever level, thinking, *This is great for me!* or *How can this person help* me? That is not the basis of a strong, healthy, or lasting relationship. Brides-to-be almost always think in terms of what a beautiful wedding *she* will have! Most of the planning is about the bride. Her dress needs to just right, and her hair needs to be done in a special way. The flowers, the table settings, and other such things are all determined to fit the whims of the bride. Our culture perpetuates the thought that the bride should think this way.

The groom also is thinking primarily in selfish terms. He is entering a relationship in which his needs and desires would be fulfilled. This new wife will be there for him, meet his needs or the needs of the home, help provide an income, as well as be available to act as a companion when they do things together. She will be someone he can lean on and find support from, someone dependable, and a joy to be with. With all these wonderful benefits, no wonder he is anxious to get married.

So they both enter a long-term commitment while believing that their personal wants and wishes will be met. Then reality sets in. When the other person fails to meet expectations, he or she is no longer seen as an asset but as a liability.

Because we seem to be living in a self-centered society, the predominant thinking is to try to fulfill *our* passions, *our* desires, and *our* hopes and dreams. When someone comes along that appears to help us along those paths, we welcome them into our lives until we realize that what they bring to the relationship is not helping us to meet our ambitions or goals. My desire to succeed is more important to me than keeping the relationship alive. The source of my disappointment is not a lack of filling my personal needs so much as it is not meeting my desires. Needs are minimal and can be filled rather easily, but desires require a higher commitment and extra effort. In order to stay on track in being fulfilled, I must rid myself of all encumbrances or distractions, including friends or mates who are dragging me down or holding me back. The cost of being self-centered is indeed high. The only workable answer to the question of how to have a relationship that works well from the moment of meeting to the (hopefully) many years of marriage is to not make it about me but to focus more on the needs and desires of our mates.

Here's John MacArthur Jr.'s take on this:

> Sacrificial love is undeserved, yet it goes to the furthest extremity—as exemplified in Christ. It says, "You don't deserve anything, but I'll give you everything. You don't deserve anything, but I'll die for you. You don't even deserve My best, but I'll give you My life." And Paul is saying [in Ephesians 5:25] that we are to say to our wives: "you may not deserve all of these things, you may be a sinner, and you may not be all that you could be—but that is never the issue. I will love you and commit myself to you, even if you are the least deserving. And I will give you everything I have … even to die for you." That's the issue!

John C. Broger, writing in a Biblical Counseling Foundation manual entitled *Self-Confrontation* (1991, page 14–6), says,

> If a believer esteems his spouse as more important than himself, he will approach solutions to any difficulties in a manner that pleases the Lord. This leads to an increasing oneness of mind and purpose as both spouses receive encouragement from Jesus Christ.

That is the point of this book. But I might add that this concept does not have to be limited to Christians. However, including the element of faith certainly adds a whole new dimension of purpose and reason to live more unselfishly.

Follow along as we look at intimate relationships before and during a marriage. Notice the differences among the attitudes, actions, and consequences of "living for me" in contrast to living for others. See how destructive it is to live selfishly. Watch how Mark and Hannah deal with the challenges of life with a godly view that says, "You are more important than I am." Then ask yourself at each step if it is like your own way of dealing with situations. Obviously, every possible condition could not be covered, simply because life is so complex that there is always an exception or any given scenario doesn't play out the way it is described here. But the point still remains that if we learn to seek the good of others over our own desires, relationships would be much improved and become a rich source of blessing. But before we discuss the interactions and attitudes within a marriage, we have to step back and see where the basis for those attitudes and actions come from. Humans are social creations so we interact on a level such that the people we relate to in our social circles have a great deal of influence on us. At the same time, we draw conclusions based on our personal observations and experiences of actions, reactions, and abnormalities within society. So the first three sections of this discussion help set the stage for what we can expect within the bonds of marriage. What happens long before the wedding day makes a huge impact on how we live after we leave the altar committed to another soul.

Before You Wed: Personal Decisions You Must Make

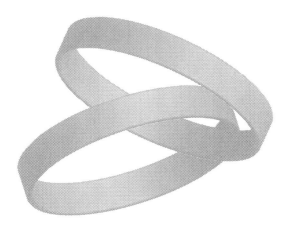

Attitudes toward Marriage

We hear all sorts of things that show how people view marriage in our world today. People's attitudes toward marriage vary. Many of them are unhealthy. Few are actually helpful. The accepted practice and the prevailing views may not always match what people feel deep in their hearts. Let's examine a few statements often heard about marriage and see what some people say about it, even if they don't really mean it.

Marriage is a form of slavery or bondage.

There are variations on this ball-and-chain idea. In whatever form it is expressed, the thought is that once a person is married, he or she loses freedom. The married man is now slave to his wife's wishes and loses the freedom to do as he pleases. The new wife is sometimes characterized as the house slave of the man. She must be ready to do what he wants when he wants it done.

I have spoken with couples who feared that this would actually happen. Usually, it is the girl who fears becoming a slave to the guy. In theory, it won't happen with the right kind of counseling and guidance. There are warning signs that potential wedding partners can watch for to prevent this from happening. It is an unhealthy relationship where one partner dominates the other. However, in our world, we know it does happen a lot, even to the point of domestic abuse.

Charles and Paige were in a close relationship for several years before they got married. Throughout the time they were together, he would often call her at home or at work just to check on what she was doing or what her plans were for the day or evening. When she tried to do something without talking to Charles first, Paige always ended up apologizing for not following his plans. As time went on, it seemed that she had less and less to say about what they would do or where they would go. Not long after they were married, he beat her badly one night because she didn't come home exactly when he thought she should. The marriage lasted less than a year. It was only after Charles was arrested that Paige had any life of her own.

It took months of therapy, prayer, and a loving family to bring her to the point where she could accept the fact that the breakup was not her fault and that Charles was not the kind of man she should be with.

David and Annmarie were married young. David came from a background of men who loved the outdoors, trucks, and rough sports. It was not unusual for him and his buddies to go off for days at a time to hunt, fish, or attend a truck rally. He saw nothing wrong with leaving his wife at home while he was away. In his mind, his love for her was expressed in his trust that she would not violate their vows while he was away.

The first year or two were fine, but after they started having children, Annmarie felt she needed more help at home and began to find excuses for David to stay at home with her and the children. There might be a need to fix the car so she would have transportation. Sometimes it was the yard that needed tending to, and she couldn't do it. As she was able to convince him a few times, she began to do it more and more often so he would be at home with her instead of going out with the boys. This was her way of claiming her rights to his time.

Over time, David gradually began to resent her demands and attitude. Arguments began to pop up, harsh words were said, and bad feelings came between them. Eventually they separated for a time, and since neither of them wanted to believe the other had a valid point, a divorce was in their future.

For Paige and David, the adage proved to be true. It seemed to them that to be married was to be a slave to the other spouse's wishes. Marriage *can* be a form of slavery, but it doesn't have to be.

Marriage is not the fairy tale it's talked up to be.

This statement too is usually said to discourage someone from entering marriage for fear of disappointment. It is true that marriage is not a state of romantic bliss that goes on day after day, year after year, without some resemblance to real life. After the honeymoon, the couple settles into a way of life with all its disagreements, difficulties, and challenges. Not every couple quickly adjusts to the new way of living. It takes time to learn things about each other. It takes time to adjust to sharing a bed, a vehicle, and household chores. There is a learning curve to master regarding finances, housing, school, jobs, and so much more. None of these things are ever mentioned in a fairy tale.

When Ralph asked Lori to marry him, he thought he was going to enjoy his life with her without serious difficulties. He understood that life has its challenges, but he was not prepared for what happened.

Lori could not keep the checkbook straight, and she couldn't handle other aspects of their finances either. Paying bills, saving for the future, and tithing were all new to her. Her parents had always done these things, so she had little or no practice. At the same time, she could not fathom why she couldn't go to a store anytime she wanted to buy things, either for herself or the home. It took a lot of time, patience, and firm discipline for Ralph to teach her how to handle their finances responsibly. Together they mastered the beast that could have ruined their marriage.

From Lori's perspective, Ralph also had a lot of learning to do. When they were first married, he would drop his dirty clothes anywhere he took them off. Rather than nagging him about it, Lori would mention how untidy the house looked, how much more work it made for her, and other such nonthreatening comments. Finally, when she saw that words were not getting through to him, she simply refused to pick up after him for a whole week. When he noticed that he was running low on T-shirts, he asked why she had not done the laundry. She simply replied, "I only wash what's in the hamper. If you want them washed, pick them up and put them there."

The differences between people and the struggles they go through do not mean that a marriage isn't a happy one or that there won't be a fairy-tale ending. There could be. When you stand back and look at the entire picture, not magnifying the details, a wonderful scene emerges.

The story is told of an artist who worked long and patiently on a painting for which he was commissioned. He anguished over the brushstrokes that didn't work exactly as he wanted. He fussed about the shades of color as he applied them to the canvas. Occasionally he would wipe out whole sections and start over because he didn't like the way it was developing. Finally, the day came to present the work of art to its owner. As he did so, the artist apologized profusely for all the mistakes he had made. The owner looked him in the eye and said, "If there were no flaws, it would not accurately reflect life. I love it!"

And so it is with marriage.

Everyone expects us to get married.

Couples who have been together for a long time certainly know a lot about each other, and if the relationship goes on, people around them begin to accept marriage as inevitable. In some situations, it would surprise us if they did *not* get married. Because we have observed them together for so long, we simply assume marriage as a natural outcome of the relationship.

Tom and Beverly knew each other in the third grade. Their parents were friends, and their families got together almost every weekend. All through their school years, they were the best of friends. In high school, they could have spent time with others of their own age but preferred each other's company. After graduation, Tom and Beverly were married in a lovely garden ceremony.

Not only was it what everyone who knew them expected, but it was what they wanted for themselves.

On the other hand, there are couples who get married because they believe it would be a great disappointment to their families and friends if it didn't happen. The fact that there is no romance or affection is set aside to give in to what is perceived as the best interest of all involved.

We see this depicted in the movies all the time. It is the sad tale of high family expectations that do not consider the feelings, hopes, and happiness of the young couple involved. We feel anger toward such people on the screen, but unfortunately, it happens all too often in real life as well. The movies do reflect real life from time to time. Those who live in social circles that see others as a lesser class do not accept outsiders easily and often have hard feelings, even hatred, toward anyone who tries to insert themselves into their family or social circle. The expectation for their children is to marry within their own socioeconomic circle.

Then there is the condition that, up until recently, people used as a reason to be married: early pregnancy. Before the cultural morals shifted so dramatically, it was always expected, even demanded, that if a young woman got pregnant, she would have to marry the father of the baby, no matter the kind of relationship between the couple. This was known as a shotgun wedding and was often the prerequisite for a troubled marriage. Blame was often put on each other, and tension was the way of life between them.

Daniel and Jessica found themselves in such a mess. They had been seeing each other only one summer when he returned to his college classes in the fall. A short time later, Jessica called to say that they were going to be parents. Because both of their parents were unhappy with this turn of events, harsh words were spoken, a flood of tears were shed, and demands were made for quick decisions. What were they going to do about the baby? Feeling that the pressure was getting too much, abortion was not an acceptable option, and the baby needed both parents to grow up, they decided to get married. After all, isn't that what their parents would do? Isn't it what some people insisted was the best solution?

To do that meant Daniel no longer qualified for some college aid programs. It also meant they would have to find jobs quickly to meet family expenses.

They took on the challenge but found that they were constantly at each other's throats, either demanding more of each other or accusing the other of being responsible for the difficult situation they were in.

A good marriage rarely comes from trying to please people outside the union.

Try it to see if you like it. If you don't, you can always get a divorce.

It's what used to be restricted to the dating scene but has been extended into the realm of marriage. This is the attitude that says there is little value in marriage, so take it or leave it. There is no plan to try to work out differences. There is no concept of permanence. There is no intention to please the other mate more than you please yourself. It is all about you.

Culturally, we have evolved to the point where this is more and more acceptable. We hear stories or even know some people who have been married multiple times, even in our churches. It is sad, but with the erosion of moral standards, it is not unexpected.

Shawn was considering asking Susan to marry him. He was not fully convinced that it was the right thing to do, considering their relationship, the timing, and other factors. When he mentioned it to some of his close friends, they all advised him that it was not such a big deal. Marriage is for some people, they said, but not for others. The only way to find out if it is for you is to try it and see. If it doesn't work out, then you'll know you made a mistake and you could get out of it easily. One of them said, "Look at me. I've been married three times. The first two didn't work out so I kept trying until found one that would stick with me—at least for now."

In years past, it was the gossip of Hollywood that so-and-so had been married several times. It was somewhat scandalous to think that would happen. Now it is as commonplace as petty thievery. It's happening all around us and to people we know personally. As a culture, we have learned to accept it as a way of life in our time.

Marriage is old-fashioned and unnecessary.

This is usually said by people who are living in a cohabitation situation. They experience companionship. They enjoy uninhibited sex. They have a relatively secure place to stay. It seems they have all the amenities of marriage without the legal document. Or do they?

This line of thinking reflects our cultural shift away from Judeo-Christian ethics. Marriage may be an old custom dating all the way back to Adam and Eve, but for too many people, it just doesn't make sense anymore.

People who cohabitate do so for a variety of reasons. They include "it makes more sense financially," "one person does not gain access to the other's fortunes," and "we just haven't gotten around to it." It is a well-known fact that many do this because they can get better benefits through federal and state assistance programs. In the minds of these people and others like them, the benefits of marriage pale in comparison to their own living arrangement, so they choose not to make their union legal or sanctified.

Tim and Tonya were such a couple. They moved in together after having known each other for only two weeks. They both had good jobs and kept their money in separate accounts. They worked out an arrangement to determine who was to pay which bills and the living expenses. A year later, they added a baby to the mix. Shortly before the baby was born, Tonya stopped working. The new situation put a lot of pressure on Tim. Would he assume full responsibility for the family or insist that Tonya take on the care of the child as well as herself with no financial support from him? Would he pressure her into going back to work as soon as possible so he could enjoy more of his own money? What about the option of applying for public assistance for housing, food, and medical care?

In the end, they worked out an adjusted arrangement that worked for them. In the whole process, not once did they consider the marriage option. They were satisfied with the way things were going, so why would they need to do that?

Those attitudes are lies or at least misconceptions. They are based on fables, bad experiences, or half truths. Because the people in our culture have strayed so far away from the God of our ancestors, there is little thought about what God thinks or says about marriage. There is a better, more positive attitude that should govern a couple's thoughts. There is no doubt that a marriage entered under the guidance and oversight of God, our Creator, is the most blessed and most sacred union that anyone can enjoy.

We always talk about marriage within the confines of our culture and convince ourselves that what is practiced among our people is the right and proper way to view marriage. Cultural shifts and changes in the moral climate influence the way people think and act. As the prevailing culture influences beliefs regarding marriage, so we behave. It is no wonder that attitudes have turned against the very institution God established so long ago.

But the fact of the matter is that the concept of marriage and the purpose for marriage were established by our Creator even before there was any human culture to bear upon the topic. Adam and Eve were not the products of an already established way of life. They were the ones to set the pattern for all who came behind to follow. God himself united them in flesh, in mind, and in spirit. When he put them together, he declared that the twofold purpose for their marriage and all marriages to follow was to be a help and support to one another and to bear offspring to populate the earth. This basic concept has been adopted in every single culture that has developed in the course of history. The God-instituted state of marriage exceeds all cultural barriers.

When two Christians marry, they are doing what God had intended in the first place. They prayerfully consider who their future mate will be and make that selection under the guidance of the Holy Spirit. When it comes time for the ceremony, they know they are entering something wonderful, something approved by God, and something that can only bring blessing and a beautiful future. A marriage that pleases the two partners is one in which there are mutual respect, mutual support, and mutual constructive criticism. That is how people grow in their relationships and as individuals. A marriage that pleases God is one that is made in heaven and lived out on earth.

Pause and Reflect

Which of these attitudes have you heard and from whom?

Do you think the person was being serious when that attitude was expressed?

Which of these attitudes most closely reflects your own feelings relating to marriage?

Do any of these attitudes contribute positively toward preparation for marriage?

What would you say is a godlier attitude and why?

Why Some Do
Not Marry

Marriage is not for everyone. Sometimes we wonder (with tongue in cheek) if a certain person who is married should have been because of their personality or circumstances. In our consideration of marriage and the wonderful blessing it can bring to those who enter it with God's guidance, we must also acknowledge that there is a segment of our population that, for one reason or another, should and will remain unmarried. In spite of the predominant view that marriage is normal and acceptable, there are some who never experience marriage. There are several reasons for this. Besides those who choose to live in cohabiting situations discussed in the previous chapter, there are at least five more reasons for remaining single in a world that emphasizes the joy of coupling up.

First, there are those who simply do not see the value of marriage over the single life. Aside from those who live in nonmarriage cohabiting arrangements, there is a class of people who enjoy being single. They love the freedom to be spontaneous. They love the independence to make personal decisions on their own. Many Christian singles find it much easier to volunteer or make time commitments than do their married counterparts. This is the kind of life Paul was talking about in 1 Corinthians 7:32–35.

My wife and I have personally known at least three women who made this choice. We are also aware of a couple of men who chose to serve the Lord as single men rather than be distracted by wives and families. For these people and many others like them, to remain single was not a bad choice. In fact, they saw it as God's will and used their freedom to serve him in ways married people could not.

Joe wanted to be a pilot from the time he was about eight or nine years old. Someone gave him a gift of a model airplane and he just fell in love with the idea of flying above the earth. His parents and friends all thought it was just a phase he would grow out of, but as time went by, he became even more thrilled about the subject, not less. In his spare time, all he wanted to study in the library or watch on videos were books and films related to flying. In high school, he worked hard at math and science so he might be accepted into a school that taught aviation. By the time he graduated, he could identify every make and model of airplane and was familiar with the cockpit layout.

During his senior year, there was a visiting missionary at a local church to which one of his friends invited him to hear. The speaker was from an aviation mission that flew to almost every corner of the globe. Joe went and decided that this was what God wanted him to do. That night he went home, read the literature he had collected, and wrote to the mission agency for a recommendation of a good aviation school.

Joe knew that to live the kind of life which required him to be away from home for long periods of time would not work well with a family. He therefore made a pledge to God that he would devote himself to the mission work and let God bring into his life a soul mate only if God wanted one for him. Forty years later, he was still single, happy, and faithfully serving the Lord with the freedom to come and go as the Spirit leads.

Joe is an example of someone who remained single by choice.

Second, there is a small group of people who, although they remain single, would love to have been married. Theirs is not a life of joy but one of disappointment and, in some cases, bitterness. As they passed through young adulthood, there just never seemed to be anyone who came into their lives that would make a good match. Their own personality may have turned away potential suitors, or the character and behaviors of the suitors were such that the couple knew it would never work well. So for these men and women, the proposal of marriage is never made and thus never responded to.

I remember a man I knew many years ago who was single his whole life. His family and friends all thought it was odd since everyone else was married or planned to be. Many of them would tease or pester him about it, saying that he was just not doing all the right things to snag a wife. I'm sure all their nagging made the matters worse for him, since he wanted to fit in, but didn't. He tried all sorts of options like going to dances, attending parties, or being at public events. Nothing worked. I heard he even tried advertising in a magazine. (This was long before online dating was even thought of.) Only once that I know of did the guy enter any kind of relationship with a woman which did not last long. Shortly after meeting, they both realized that marriage between them was not a good option. Her background was totally different from his. Each held different expectations of the other. She was from an urban environment, and he was from the sticks. She was well educated; he barely passed the eighth grade. She loved money; he had none. You get the picture. There was no common ground from which to base a relationship long term. After they parted, he gave up on the idea of marriage and died a single, lonely man.

Marjorie too felt the pressure of being involved in some kind of relationship, except the results were different. She longed to be married and have a family. She had developed a deep, intimate relationship with one man, so she really thought this was going to happen. They seemed to hit it off and loved each other's company. When they were not at their respective jobs, they were together. This went on for several months. As soon as it became known that she was pregnant, the man disappeared and left her on her own. Unfortunately for her, the end of the relationship was having a child but not gaining a husband. As a single mom, she knew her chances for marriage were diminished greatly. All the while she was raising her child, she was bitter toward men. That bitterness played out in her relationships with her family, friends, and others. Everyone knew she was not in favor of romance at all. Even now, after her child has grown into adulthood, she still harbors bad feelings toward members of the opposite gender.

Both of these cases show that though some people would love to join the ranks of the happily married, circumstances—or fate as some would call it—stepped in and shut the door.

The third possible reason is the result of some people's high expectations in a spouse. They may enjoy a great relationship with someone of the opposite gender, but when the question is popped, they react negatively. They say no and then list all the reasons why the guy doesn't measure up to her standards. Perhaps he is fun to be with but quite irresponsible in his behavior. Maybe he is responsible on the job but a weekend alcoholic. Whatever the criteria are, no one ever seems to quite fit the bill.

I remember watching a movie once with this thought as its theme. As the story unfolds, the woman rejects one lover after another because they didn't match her quality list. That is, until someone came into her life that she just couldn't resist loving back. All her resolve, all her planning, and most of her listed requirements went out the window when love entered the room.

I understand that sociologists have determined that many men will hold up their mothers as a model for the wife they seek. This is because she is the one who has nurtured him, fed him, and listened to him when he needed someone to talk to. In his mind, his mother is the best example of a good wife. So when he interacts with women in his own age group, he mentally compares them to his mother, either consciously or unconsciously. When they don't seem to measure up to his standards, he moves on to the next possible candidate.

Gary was like that. He was from a good home, and his parents dearly loved each other and their children. Gary's dad was away a lot, so he spent most of his formative years in the company of his mother, admiring her for her skills as nurse, counselor, teacher, friend, and mom. So when it came time for Gary to start dating, he looked for someone who would not force him out of his comfort zone but would carry on the same or similar environment he grew up in. They were very difficult shoes to fill. In Gary's case, they never were. No one ever seemed to be just right.

For those people (usually women) who reject the offer of

marriage, the reasons are legitimate and good in their own minds. Whether or not they are in reality is another matter. Perhaps their standards are unrealistically high. Perhaps they are even a little bit quirky (like the lady who would only date men with red hair). In any case, the result is they end up living alone.

The fourth reason is related to the third except the rejection is more general and all-inclusive. A woman has a few dates with men who seem initially to be good prospects for future husbands. However, the men turn out to be rude, disrespectful, or perhaps abusive in language, attitudes, and actions. Because they have had only bad experiences with a few men, these women write off all men as undesirable and would rather remain single than risk going through such abuse and lingering pain again.

Jackie was such a woman. When she was a college student, she went out with a few men from her college. None of the men she dated treated her well. A couple of them even tried to take advantage of her sexually. After one particularly bad episode where she was beaten and nearly raped, she determined that enough was enough. No more men would ever get close to her again. She has remained single all her life and feels bitterness and pain that go deep into her heart. For her and women like her, marriage is out of the question. Her trust in men has been broken so many times it would take a miracle to build that up again.

Jackie is not alone. Many other women have had similar experiences with comparative results. Women like Jackie live a single life out of fear of intimacy and legitimately so.

Finally, there is that group of individuals who will remain unmarried through no fault of their own. They have physical or mental handicaps that prevent the necessary social interaction that is a prerequisite for marriage. God in his wisdom has allowed them to be victims of disease, accident, or deformity to such a degree that it would be unwise or impossible for them to be united with another soul in a situation of mutual accountability. Since they cannot function at the level where they understand or are able to be responsible for themselves, they would not be able to accept responsibility for someone else, which marriage demands.

Almost every community has such people. They are in our group homes. They meet together for therapy or at activity centers.

They are on our streets and in our schools, churches, and homes. These handicapped citizens come from all walks of life and every level of income. We see them everywhere. Perhaps you know one or more of them. These people are single because logistically marriage would never work for them.

Remaining single then is sometimes by choice and sometimes not. Whatever the reason, we must acknowledge that there is a portion of our world population that will never experience marriage. In a world that celebrates marriage, let us also be mindful of those who for one reason or another remain single. Do not think you *have* to get married. It is more important to follow God's will than to be married and be disobedient.

Pause and Reflect

How many singles do you know?

Have they ever been married?

Why have those who have never been married not done so?

Do you know anyone personally who has issues with the concept of marriage?

Do you know anyone personally who has been hurt by a relationship and rejects marriage?

Are any of the reasons stated above godly reasons? If so, which ones?

Have you or your potential spouse ever been hurt in a relationship such that it causes anxiety or fear about getting married?

Dating

Has dating become outdated? With outside influences, with new generations being more one world in their thinking, and with shifting attitudes toward religion and the Bible in particular, our culture in America and the West is changing before our eyes. In spite of the changes that are happening, however, one cultural practice that has been in effect for centuries is refusing to die: the steps toward and preparations for marriage.

Marriage itself is as old as humankind. It was first introduced in the garden to Adam and Eve. It has been a part of human society ever since, although different people in various parts of the world use different methods of sealing the marriage or performing the ceremony.

In our Western culture, the marriage ceremony is usually preceded by an engagement period of varying lengths, which in turn, is preceded by the question. Even the question is not really the first step because before that, most couples will spend a period of time getting to know one another in a process called dating.

It is unfortunate that our culture has shifted in such a way that dating is not practiced with the same level of dignity and respect that it used to be. Many couples now go right from an introduction to a few dates or meetings to living together. But let's examine the value of a respectful, dignified dating process that would help make a future marriage work.

The process is as simple as it is practical. One individual, usually the guy, will ask the girl if she would like to go with him to an event. It could be a dance, a school play, a football game, a movie, or some other public venue. This is the first step in finding out likes and dislikes. Does she like me well enough to go with me? Does she like the kind of event I am asking her to go to? Each subsequent date, if there are more, will increase the knowledge each has of the other.

Not only will they discover likes and dislikes, they will also gain an understanding of each other's personalities and habits. She may discover that he is proud, arrogant, and sometimes rude to people. He may learn that she is spoiled and wants everything done for her and her way. Sometimes their two personalities click, but more often than not, they clash and the two end up going their separate ways. It is not unusual for a young person to date several members of the opposite gender before finding one they believe they can live with in a sense of harmony for life.

I distinctly remember a time when I was a freshman in college and a mutual friend thought I might hit it off with a girl on campus. I called her, and she agreed to meet me for lunch. It was probably the most awkward lunch I had ever sat through at that point in my life. We were both somewhat shy and didn't know what to say or the right questions to ask. It ended with us both agreeing that there probably was not a future for us as a couple. After that, it took four or five more attempts before I met the woman God had in mind for me. Some relationships were brief, only one or two dates, a couple of them lasted for a few months, but in the end, we parted, usually on mutual and friendly terms.

How a person conducts himself or herself on a date is indicative of how he or she will act later in life. If a young man has been taught by his parent(s) to show respect to the woman he is with, he will continue to show respect to his future wife. If, however, he does not offer to hold the door, does not try to please her with the best choice of places to eat or the meal ordered, he will disregard her likes and dislikes later on as well. If a woman does not let her date know what she expects from him by way of courtesy or is rude and mouthy to him all the while they are together, she will probably turn out to be a nagging wife he would do well to avoid. On the other hand, if she shows genuine thankfulness for his attention to her and expresses gratitude for gestures he makes to try to please her, she will, more than likely, be a wife who supports and encourages her husband as they grow together in the marriage process.

I have known young men who, when out with a girl, show them no more courtesy than taking a dog for a walk. They never open a door, they seldom walk at her side in a protective mode, and they do not respect her wishes relating to the kind of place they go or the things they do together. It is usually what he wants to do, and he brings her along. She tags along to be seen as being attached and submits to his choices. Before long, he begins demanding her to cater to him in more than just being there. She can run for the food; she can buy the tickets; she can make the reservations. This could have all been avoided if the girl in this case had stood her ground early on and refused additional dates with someone who treated her so disrespectfully. It is better to be single and happy than attached and unhappy.

In contrast is the college student who sets up a date with a coed and at the first meeting they talk casually about their classes, the school, and other things they have in common. He asks polite and interesting questions and listens intently to her answers. She in turn asks him about the things she considers important and learns where he stands on certain social issues. Together they spend more time than they had planned just getting to know each other a little bit. When it came time to part, he saw that she made it back to her room safely and they agreed that they would like to do it again. There was no pressure, no demands, and no expectations other than a possible second date.

The dating ritual, if handled properly, can be a valuable tool for anyone to use to help determine whom it is that God has in store for them as a future mate in the bond of marriage. It should not be abused to try to find a slave girl to provide for you. It should never be used as a means of finding a rich husband, whether or not he loves you. Dating is not a method of finding a good sex partner. The tool of dating is really using a gift of our culture to weed out persons who may look attractive on the surface but are undesirable mates when you get to know them even a little. That doesn't mean they are not marriage material. It simply means they are not the person God has for you. It is an investigative tool. People use it to discover the character, the quality, and the details of another person to help decide where this relationship is going.

Ray, a senior in high school, had dated several girls before he started seeing Linda. By the time he was ready to ask her out, he had learned some things that worked and some things that didn't as far as impressing the girls. For example, he found out early that most girls do not want to be rushed in a relationship. When he tried to kiss one of his dates on their first meeting, he received a firm slap and a memory of being greatly embarrassed. With Linda, he asked what she wanted to do, and they agreed on a place and time. He opened doors, asked what she wanted off the menu and ordered for her, and basically put her needs and interests ahead of his own. They hit it off, and the relationship lasted all through college, after which they were married on the anniversary of their first date.

Allen too had taken several girls on dates. With him, however, the goal was not to seek a mate but to find someone to "have fun with." He wanted a girl who was a little bit wild, a little bit rebellious, or willing to push the envelope in regard to rules. When he met Jennifer, he found the girl of his dreams and the two of them did some crazy things together. That all ended one night in an auto accident as a result of drinking and driving.

Mark and Hannah's case is different. Both of them had pledged themselves to a life of submission to God. When they met in college, one of the first questions they asked of each other was "What is your relationship with God like?" From that, they built a bond of mutual friendship, a vision of mission in the world, and a love that would see them through whatever life would throw at them. It was not long into their series of dates that they both realized God had brought them together.

For each of these couples, dating proved useful. It proved its worth in helping them to decide whom to maintain a relationship with and whom to let go. But as we have seen, the ultimate purpose was, in all but Mark and Hannah's, a selfish and shallow one. Theirs was the only one of the cases cited that had a higher goal in mind: to serve God in all things, even their marriage.

A marriage made in heaven must begin by taking godly, biblical steps here on earth. Anyone desiring God's blessing and guidance on their marriage must be obedient to God's teaching on relationships right from the start. And we know from 1 Corinthians 13:5, "Love is not self-seeking."

Pause and Reflect

What have your dating experience(s) been like?

Can you see yourself in any of the characters depicted above?

How did the dating experience help you process your attitudes or feelings toward the opposite gender?

Can a person find a suitable marriage partner without going through the dating process? If so, how?

In your opinion, how long should a couple see each other on dates before making a serious commitment?

Does family influence make a difference to you about who you date?

When the Bible says we should honor (respect) our parents. Does that mean we should listen to them concerning who we spend time with on dates?

Premarital Intimacy

The desire for sex can ruin a relationship. It can also destroy lives.

Paul was typical college student with the ambition of becoming a lawyer. He attended a prestigious university and was getting good grades. At the same time that he was pursuing his education, he was also chasing the ladies to try to find someone who could meet his personal, emotional, and sexual needs and desires. After dating several girls on campus, he met Penny, who worked as an office manager in a local business. They seemed to hit it off and saw each other often. Paul appreciated the way Penny was so patient when he wanted to talk about his classes, his professors, or his dreams to become a lawyer. She would usually encourage him to see things in a long-range perspective and not focus on the temporary struggles or hardships. Late one night, in her apartment, after a long hard day for both of them, he was very tired and emotionally drained. Instead of getting up to go to his own residence, he suggested that he might spend the night with her. He used the argument that he might fall asleep on the way and it would be her fault if he were to get into an accident. Paul was playing two cards in hopes of winning the pot. Sympathy for his state of tiredness and the danger of driving in such a condition was one. That alone could have been enough, considering Penny's own vulnerability to give in to her desires. The other card was guilt.

He wanted Penny to believe that if there were to be an accident, it could have been prevented by her simply saying it was okay for him to spend the night.

Penny now has a decision to make. She can let him stay and attempt to meet his sexual desire, which was clearly intimated, or she could send him away and keep her own similar desires in check. She did not have to give in to his lame tactics, but the temptation was too great. Her own sexual urges were such that this was an opportunity to be fulfilled herself. Paul could meet *her* needs as well as she could help him. So that night, they were both temporarily satisfied.

Now they had taken the step into intimacy, there was a bond between them that could either be strengthened or broken. As long as they were both getting what they wanted out of the relationship, they would continue on. There was no guilt, no remorse, and no shame. He could do his studies ambitiously, then go to her and be fulfilled relationally and sexually. She could work all day and meet him in the evening to spend time with such an incredible man. Her loneliness would be gone as well as her longing to be loved. It was not long before they moved in together.

Neither of them saw what was coming.

In his third year of college, Paul was required to spend time visiting courtrooms and meeting with practicing lawyers to get a feel of what it was like in the real world outside of class. That meant many evenings at board meetings or at clubs rubbing elbows with people in the legal world. Some of this was required by his professors, and part of it was voluntary. These activities were in addition to the late hours of study he did at home. Penny was left alone more than she cared to be. His pursuit of a career began to push her to the bottom of his agenda. Anger and resentment began to set in, and the fights became more and more frequent. Eventually things came to a head and they broke up. They went their separate ways, her with a broken heart and him with a freedom to carry on without the hindrance and distraction she had become to him.

Shortly after their breakup, Penny discovered that she was pregnant. Now she had no man who cared for her, a child on the way, and the distinct feeling that she had failed somehow. Her personal goals of being married and settling down with a loving husband had been shattered. She was not sure she could ever trust any man again. Nor was she sure how she could manage raising a child on her own. One thing was for sure. This child she was carrying would be a serious detriment to everything she had dreamed and worked for. Staying on her career path of owning her own business just became very complicated. How she would deal with this new situation is the question she wrestled with for a long time. She knew that she really had three choices. She could bring the child to birth and struggle trying to rear it on her own as a single mom, she could give it birth and place it up for adoption and thus be free of any obligation to it, or she could find a clinic that would just make it go away permanently.

Because she was intent on her career and future goals, the first option seemed to be out of the question. She would have to put up with all the office gossip, the personal decisions relating to the birth, and end up with a minimum eighteen-year sentence to motherhood she did not want. Not now at least. The second option was not much better for her. There would still be the gossip, the rejection, and the feeling of being left out of things because of her "condition." She didn't know if she could stand that for nine months. In both of these situations, the loneliness would have been intensified, knowing that she had the attention of a man, but it had escaped her, possibly condemning her to live singly. In both cases, it would mean she would have to take the focus of her life off herself and direct it toward her child for a time. The last choice seemed to be the best option. It would free her from the swelling belly, the pain of childbirth, and any final attachments to Paul, who by now had forgotten all about her. It was, for her, the best decision to make to keep her on her path to success.

"Living for me" has cost Paul the love of a good woman and the chance to be a father to his child. "Living for me" has cost Penny the relationship she had with Paul, her own self-respect, and the life of her unborn baby. Self-centeredness leaves fallout wherever it is present. Hurt feelings, damaged relationships, and even death follow when we exercise our selfish desires. Like a severe storm that passes through, "living for me" leaves a trail of destruction, and no matter what you do, you can never go back to the way it was before the storm.

Mark too was ambitious. He had determined early in life that he would do what he could to make a difference in the lives of others. After high school, he went on to college to study to be a doctor. That meant a lot of late nights studying and practicing. Often he would drag himself into bed at two or three in the morning only to get up again a five o'clock to start another long day. It was exhausting, but his eye was on the goal and the suffering seemed to be worth it.

Somewhere along the way, at one of the many group sessions he attended, Hannah came into his life. She was bright, cheerful, and full of energy. Whenever they were together, they enjoyed each other's company. He learned that Hannah was at the school to become a pediatric nurse. She loved children and wanted to be someone who could help them with physical or medical needs. He shared with her that he also wanted to make a difference but had not settled on any specific area of medicine. Since they shared some of their classes together, they decided it might be a good idea to meet regularly in the library to study. So they did.

This went on for two years. As they continued to meet, study, and talk, they were drawn to each other and the relationship became more than a study session. Mark liked the way Hannah encouraged and supported him in his studies. Often she would work with him to understand topics or areas of study that seemed difficult for him. She also encouraged him to get more rest for his own health. She seemed to be genuinely interested in him for his sake, not her own. She often forfeited her time to study just to help him cope with his own struggles. The day he got the news that his Dad had had a stroke was extra special. Not only did she weep with him, but she offered to drive him home if he wanted so he could be with his family. That showed him how much she really cared, not about herself or her career but for him. He understood then what love was all about.

On Mark's part, the goal he had in life was not to be a doctor for the sake of being a doctor. He wanted to be a doctor who made a difference. After getting to know Hannah and seeing how unselfish she was, he determined that he would be like that as well. In one of his many discussions with her, he asked her what area of study she thought he should pursue as a specialty. Her answer, after a little hesitation, was simple. "Follow your heart. What do you believe God has gifted you with? Is it toward children as he has me or to some other aspect of medicine? Only you can really answer that."

He thought about that for a long, long time. Finally the answer came to him. He would try to be a family doctor so he could help people of all ages with their medical needs. He could assist in the birth of children, the scrapes, bruises, and diseases of childhood, and the maladies of middle and old age. He could become the friendly doc who cares about the entire family. That would also fit well with Hannah's plans, if the Lord should allow them to become a team.

When he shared his decision with Hannah, she was overjoyed. She was excited for him because he could now concentrate on the necessary studies for future practice, and she was excited that he cared enough about her future to possibly include her in them.

One night after they had finished their usual study session, Mark suggested that they go somewhere to eat. When they had finished their meal, which they both thoroughly enjoyed, he mentioned that there was a movie being shown on campus that he wanted to see. Would she want to come along? Hannah gracefully declined, saying that she had to go home the next day to see her parents. She had promised that whenever she could get away on a weekend that she would come to spend time with her mother, who was dying of cancer. He understood and walked her to her apartment. As they were saying good night, he asked if she was sure she didn't want him to come in and keep her company. The impending death of a loved one could be so emotionally draining. She said thank-you, but no. Even though her desire was to have him hold her and comfort her, she realized that one night of intimacy could cost them both dearly.

When she returned to campus on Monday, Mark went to Hannah, and after hearing how her weekend went, he apologized to her for the way he acted on Friday night. She accepted his apology, saying that she understood and the feeling was mutual, but to follow their respective dreams, they could not afford to get distracted by selfish temporary desires. He agreed.

In this case, there was no "living for me." Each of the two was more interested in the needs and desires of the other. And because there was a growing respect for each other, there were no regrets, no hard feelings, and no shame in what they were doing. This couple was on their way to a long, happy, and fulfilled relationship.

Even though they had not yet talked about marriage, they both knew the potential was there and the bond they had might lead to that. They also knew that marriage would have to wait until at least one of them was out of school. To be married and try to keep up with the demands of two college schedules, develop a source of income, and potentially start a family at this point was not sensible or practical. For the next couple of years, at least, they would have to be content to spend as much time together as their busy schedules allowed. Mark understood that he needed to keep his mind focused on his studies. Hannah realized that to be prepared for what they both expected, she too needed to focus on the things at hand and get not caught up in dreaming about the future. What they both wanted for themselves would have to wait.

Pause and Reflect

Which of your friends do you know have been sexually active before marriage?

Why do you think they give in to their sexual desire?

Has anyone you know become pregnant as a result? What was the outcome?

Has your own sexual desire caused you to participate in such activity?

How did you feel afterward?

The Bible teaches that we should keep ourselves sexually pure before marriage. Why do think God considers that important?

How does keeping yourself sexually pure reflect on your desire to give your future spouse the best that you have?

Coming Together as One

The Proposal

O ur culture still applauds a marriage proposal, especially one made in a unique or public manner. There is joy in knowing that two people desire to spend the rest of their lives together in harmony. We cheer them on and hope the best for them. In spite of statistics that might say otherwise, we want them to succeed and live a long and happy life together.

The couple has been together for a while, and now they feel they are ready to take the relationship further. At some point, one of them (usually the man) decides that this is the person he wants to live with on a permanent basis. So he asks the all-important question "Will you marry me?"

Of all the wedding proposals I have witnessed, both in real life and on the screen, it seems that no matter how long the couple has been together, that moment when the biggest question of a woman's life is asked seems full of joy, excitement, and thrill, the likes of which nothing else can compare. It is the highlight of her life up to this point.

As a couple, this one question anticipates several things for them. There are things they cannot experience alone and in some cases cannot be shared by anyone who is not married.

First of all, they can look forward to a lifetime of companionship. For two people who enter such a relationship, it means there will always be someone there for them in times of need. When one of them comes home tired after a long day at work, it is pleasing to know there is a shoulder to lean on and a friend to talk to. Companionship also means that whatever life brings your way, you will share the experience with someone who cares, who encourages, and who helps guide you through the process.

Companionship is related to the meeting of personal relationship needs. We all have them. No one is intended to live alone. We need others to bounce our ideas off of. We need others to listen to our gripes, our venting of anger, or our joyous excitement over the good things in life. It is pleasant to know that there is a person we can depend on to share birthdays, special events, and other life milestones with. Those are all a part of relational needs. A good marriage partner will certainly help fulfill those needs.

Mike and Julie learned the value of companionship early in their marriage. Mike worked in an office and sometimes didn't get home until after 6 p.m. Julie also worked but was able to be there early enough to have dinner ready by the time Mike arrived. After dinner, the two of them would just relax on the couch and talk. Sometimes it would be about work. Other times they would discuss what was going on with their friends, family, or neighbors. For Mike and Julie, the after-dinner hour was the most rewarding part of the day because they both knew that the other would be there for them to talk to and unwind. Even after they had been married for a long time, they continued their after-dinner talks. For them it was as important as any part of their relationship.

Then there were Peter and Pat. Peter had strong relational needs. He grew up in a broken home, not knowing his father. Because his mother had to work all day to provide for the family, he never got to spend quality time with her either. So Peter essentially grew up alone. As an adult, he knew he needed a wife he could cling to for help, for friendship, and just to be there when he needed her for anything. Pat was such a wife. Having grown up in a stable home environment, Pat brought a sense of strength to the marriage that Peter needed. On the other hand, Peter would go out of his way to be supportive of Pat, knowing the hurts, the pain, and the mental anguish of rejection and being ignored. This couple knew that relational needs are very important and cannot be overlooked. To do so would jeopardize the marriage.

Thirdly, on a more practical level, when we have a good spouse, we know we have someone who will support, encourage, and help us with decisions that have to be made. "He who finds a wife finds what is good" (Proverbs 18:22). The same thing can be said in reverse. Finding a husband is also a good thing. We do have to qualify that, however, and say a *good* spouse because marrying the first person to come along will not work out well. We all know from experience some of the things that require serious discussion between spouses. Buying a home versus renting, the choice of which vehicle to own, job opportunities, birthing of children, schooling, and so many more are things we all wish we had an expert on our side to help us with. Our spouses may not be experts, but just to have them there adds confidence to the decision-making process. So a good spouse is a valuable asset in the decision-making process.

The fourth item that a newly married couple can look forward to is sexual satisfaction. Many people put this at the top of the list, but no matter where it is in priority, it should be mentioned that a good marriage partner will also be a good bed partner. That is because the giving attitude that should be evident between the couple should clearly be evident in the bedroom. Each one should be willing to give of themselves for the satisfaction of the other. A good marriage is never about what I want but what I can do to satisfy my partner. Demanding things from your spouse to fulfill desires or fantasies usually does not end well. The partner feels used, abused, or at the least reluctant to participate. Being self-focused in the bedroom does not show respect for the other person's emotions, physical well-being, or mental state. There may be good reasons to say no at this time. Finding a good partner is important for the sexual side of marriage as well as any other aspect of it.

Millions of men and women, including me, would love to have known this long before they became intimately involved with a partner. Unfortunately, our culture has brainwashed us into thinking sex is all about being personally satisfied. We are trained to ask, "What will satisfy me?" Advertising agencies use this ploy all the time to sell their goods and services. *I want* because it will satisfy me. *I will get* because it will please me. That same mentality affects the way we view our partners or potential partners. How satisfying will he or she be in bed? Will he or she meet my selfish desires as often and in the ways I want?

For a longer-lasting relationship, especially in a marriage, the very opposite is what we should be practicing. What can I do to please my partner? How can we develop a loving, caring atmosphere in our home to the degree that our time in the bedroom would be not so much erotic as it is mentally and physically satisfying, knowing that our partner was pleased with us? A good sex life is a shared satisfaction.

Mark and Hannah approached the matter of commitment in a less impulsive way. After two years of studying together, spending free time together, and just being there for each other, Mark asked Hanna to marry him. It was no surprise to Hanna and she immediately said yes. Once they had made the verbal commitment to God and to each other, they intentionally brought up the subjects that needed to be discussed, such as the date of the wedding, the location, and the guest list. They both knew and accepted the fact that this was too important to rush into and that with their busy schedules it was much better to take their time and plan this once-in-a-lifetime event well.

After considering all of these things, it is safe to say that the joy of being asked to marry someone, knowing that it is a good match, will generate thoughts of a life together that is characterized by peace, comfort, and happiness. That is not to say there will not be times of struggle, strife, and turmoil but that the general tone of their life together can be seen as tranquil. In the spirit of the moment, all negative thoughts are pushed away or forgotten. It is with the idea of a positive future that she will say yes!

Pause and Reflect

What is the best proposal you have witnessed or heard about?

What was the most unique?

How have some proposals you know about reflect a truly personal situation?

What would you like your own proposal experience to be like?

If you have already reached that point in your relationship, what was it like? Was it unique, personal, or just matter-of-fact?

Even if you were in a long-term relationship, did the proposal make a difference in that relationship?

The Engagement Period

From the moment the question is asked until the day of the wedding ceremony is a period of formal commitment. The ancients referred to this as the betrothal period. More recently in our Western culture, we call it the time of engagement. In either case, it means that the couple has entered a new level in their relationship than before. They have now declared to the entire world—well, at least to everyone who knows them—that they are fully committed to each other and that at some later date they will become husband and wife.

For the couple, it means that each has declared his or her loyalty to the other and there is no plan or reason to even think seriously about dating or seeing anyone else romantically. For them the decision has been made, and they intend to stick with it.

Now that the tension has been relieved regarding whether or not they will be married, there is a new feeling in the air. It is a feeling of anticipation. When will the wedding be?

Each couple must decide for themselves how long the engagement period will last. Some are very short, lasting only a few days. Others stretch into months and years. I have seen both extremes.

Roy and Kim were married as soon as possible after making the commitment. They were engaged on a Friday and got married on Monday. It was simple affair with the justice of the peace officiating. A couple of friends were there to act as witnesses. Quick, easy, and simple was the way they wanted it. Family members only found out later.

With George and Carol, it was just the opposite. They got engaged shortly after graduating from college. It has now been almost fifteen years and they still have not set a date. Careers, ambitions, and other excuses keep delaying what they committed themselves to doing. They just haven't felt ready to take their relationship to the next level. They have fallen into the trap we discussed in an earlier chapter about not seeing the value of marriage when they have all they want without the certificate.

Being committed, however, brings a certain level of responsibility. For an engaged couple, it should bring to them the exclusive responsibility of making each other happy and learning to be responsible for the welfare of their intended mate. Being responsible means looking for adequate housing, sharing decision-making, anticipating large purchases, handling combined finances, and the entire list of other things couples share. Learning to do these things while engaged allows them to learn how each handles stress and see how the other person reacts to deadlines and balancing a checkbook or credit card account. These processes can really teach someone a lot about someone else.

A man can really please his fiancée in practical and helpful ways. One way is to show that he is willing and actually wants to help around the house. That doesn't mean just taking out the trash. If he wants to please his future wife, it means he will learn to help with the laundry, washing the dishes, and vacuuming the rugs. It means he will do what it takes to help her get the work done so they spend quality relaxing time together. It means taking responsibility to see that her car is maintained and property is kept up, not making her continue to do that because she always did before you were married. It means learning to put her first in the relationship.

A woman can please her man by not using housework as an excuse to separate herself from activities that he does in the garage, on the lawn, or wherever his chores may take him. She should learn to run the lawn mower, rake leaves, or trim the hedge. The future wife could help make the grounds a little more beautiful by planting flowers or shrubbery. She can walk the dog, take the cat to the vet, or detail his car when she does her own. Loving him means putting him first in her life.

They both could be supportive in their respective careers. The last thing a working person wants to hear when he or she comes home is criticism for not having time for the spouse or fiancé. For many people, their work creates an identity for them and to have it demeaned or criticized is hard to take. Being informed about each other's work responsibilities and being there to listen without judging is a valuable asset to the relationship.

Dan worked long hours in construction and would come home exhausted after a day of hard work. Shortly after arriving home, he would receive a call from Kristie, his fiancée. She would talk a few minutes and then inquire what plans he had for the evening. She was hoping he would take her out somewhere. She also worked but had a much more relaxing job with few demands on her physically. So when she called, she would be ready to go do something for an hour or two. Dan didn't have that kind of energy left at the end of a workday, so more times than not, he would try to beg off. Kristie was looking out for her own pleasures and not really caring about Dan's feelings. She would often berate him for not wanting to do the things she wanted. She could not identify with the level of fatigue Dan was experiencing.

As a doctor in training, Mark also had very long hours at work. His was a hectic schedule of hospital rounds, clinic appointments, study time, conferences, and constantly interacting with other people. By the time he arrived back at his apartment, all he wanted to do was relax. After unwinding for a little while, he would call Hannah or go meet her somewhere just to talk over the events of the day. They would hear each other's stories, vent their frustrations, and offer support and encouragement to each other. Each of them was deeply interested in what was going on in their daily lives and truly wanted to help in any way possible. They were there for each other. There were no selfish demands or thinking that one's life is more important than the other's.

When it comes to children, they should learn that it is

both parents' responsibility to rear them in a home of love, companionship, and a caring attitude. For him it is not a matter or passing the buck off to the mom. For her it is not trying to force them off on him at the end of a workday when he is as tired as she is. It is working together to nourish, train, and lead these young lives through the struggles of life by using unselfish attitudes and means.

In other words, when it comes to making a future spouse happy, each one needs to do those things we learn that will make life a little easier for the other. Love is not letting someone else carry the entire load while you take it easy. Love is not doing everything for someone else that they could be doing for themselves. Love is sharing: sharing the load, sharing the joys, and sharing the desire to serve one another.

But whether the engagement period is long or short, the goal is to one day be officially married. While they are waiting for the wonderful day to arrive, they live with an air of expectancy. Something good is on the horizon.

For those whose engagement period lasts longer than a year, some even multiple years, there is the balancing effect of negative circumstances. Just as in a married life, engaged couples experience setbacks and difficulties along the way to the altar. There are disappointments that have to be overcome. There are disagreements that have to be resolved. There are changes in their circumstances that have to be dealt with. And whether or not they will admit it, there may also be temptations to be resisted.

One couple was engaged in May and had planned a wonderful wedding for the fall. During the summer, the man suffered a broken leg and couldn't work. With a limited income, they could not afford the big wedding they had planned or the honeymoon trip they had hoped to take. It was a big disappointment to them, but it did not stop them from going through with their wedding. It was just scaled back and their honeymoon was spent at a national park instead of Europe.

Many couples disagree about where they should live after the wedding. Should it be near his parents, her parents, or somewhere else? If this is not worked out early, it could be a major point of contention during the engagement period. Disagreements arise over many other things besides housing, like careers, schooling, children, and so much more. While they are committed to each other and waiting to tie the knot, they have a great opportunity to work through all the things they may not agree on. This is a perfect time to work on being unselfish by listening carefully to each other and considering all sides of the issue and coming to a mutual agreement as to what the best solution for them is.

Changes in their personal, financial, or career circumstances can really set a couple back if they let them. Being stricken with a debilitating disease would alter their total situation and may cause them to reassess their future together. If their love is deep enough and strong enough, the challenge will be overcome, but it will not be easy. This was so well described in the hit movie *Love Story* a few years ago. The wife was diagnosed with terminal cancer shortly after the wedding and the husband would not give up on her or the relationship.

Loss of a job or just changing careers can cause financial hardships that become the center of arguments, heated discussions, or at least late-night worries. When a couple has made plans based on a known regular income and that income is suddenly cut, it changes everything. The question "What are we going to do?" rings off walls in many homes when this happens. It is a measure of their commitment when a couple works together to find a creative solution to handle the issue rather than fight and argue about it.

In our culture of freedom, including the freedom to spend time with whomever you want, there is the extremely high risk of sexual temptation. This is never truer than when there is no set date or the engagement period has dragged on for years with no resolution in sight. It is also a high-risk situation when one of the partners is called into active military duty and there is a physical separation as well as a weakening emotional connection. I have heard of many relationships that been broken by the distance factor. While one is away for military duty or on business in some far away location, it is so easy to find comfort in the arms of someone else. The affair may start out innocently enough as just spending time with a friend. Those visits then, however unintentionally, become more frequent and more intimate until they wake up at some point and realize that it has developed into a real marriage breaker. These kinds of temptations are not restricted to engaged couples, to be sure, but they are another matter of great concern that couples who have pledged themselves must be aware of and try to deal with because the temptation may be real for one or the other of them.

Setbacks can and do happen. Because of them, many couples fall apart and the engagement is broken off. But for those couples who have a higher level of commitment, for those who take the time to work through issues and difficulties, the goal is the same and has not been changed by circumstances. They still want to spend the rest of their lives with the one they have chosen or they believe God has chosen for them. For them, the hardships have only made the commitment stronger. They are still living with anticipation for the day they are joined as husband and wife.

Pause and Reflect

What is the longest engagement period you are aware of?

The shortest?

How long do you anticipate yours to be?

Was this discussed beforehand with your partner?

How flexible are you with the length of your engagement?

What kinds of circumstances might cause you to shorten it or lengthen it?

What might cause you or your intended spouse to call it off?

If it were called off, how would that affect your relationship with God since you thought he brought you two together?

The Union

The day you have been waiting anxiously for has finally arrived. This is your wedding day! You and your partner have planned and prepared for this moment with great care to detail and décor. You have invited everyone whom you wished could be there. You have worked with friends and family to prepare a lavish feast to feed all those in attendance, and the two of you are now ready to stand up in public to declare your loyalty to each other by taking vows that are never meant to be broken.

In our Western culture, the ceremony is usually elegant and festive. The church or civic hall is decorated with streamers and flowers. The groom dresses in a nice suit or tuxedo; the bride wears a dress especially chosen for the occasion. Other members of the party also dress in clothes meant to make the event more special in recognition of the couple and their happiness.

The ceremony itself can be short and simple or lengthy and elaborate. Many couples include a special song either sung by a soloist or played over a speaker system. Some include other family members in the ceremony; others do not. They include family as a part of the reception to follow. Many couples use flower girls and a ring bearer. The ones who choose not to use them have the best man or the maid of honor perform those duties. In any case, the ceremony is tailored to fit the needs and the desires of the couple being united together by this sacred event.

Andrew and Christine chose to have a simple wedding. There were no special songs or fancy decorations. They invited everyone to their local church, where their pastor performed the ceremony simply by reading the parts from a book and pronouncing them husband and wife. They chose not to have a flower girl or ring bearer. In fact, Andrew carried the rings in his suit jacket pocket and fished them out at the proper time.

Stan and Brandy went all out. They had the resources and the network of family and friends that allowed them to use the biggest church in town, hire a musician and singer, and dress the wedding party in clothes that most people would have to pay a month's wages to wear. For them, it was worth the expense for this very special day in their lives. There were three flower girls in procession, followed by a young boy carrying a special pillow, color coordinated with the wedding theme, who bore the rings tied to the pillow with a pretty bow. At the appropriate time, he passed the pillow to the groom to remove a ring and make his vow. He then offered the pillow to the bride to repeat her portion of the vows. The whole ceremony was well rehearsed and performed, not unlike any stage performance from a script.

However, for both couples, there was one thing they had in common. In the end, they were united as husband and wife for time to come. No more living singly or with the uncertainty of the permanence of their relationship. They were now one: one in union, one in purpose, and one in mind and in soul. Now they would face the world as one.

Every formal wedding that I have witnessed has that one special moment when the doors open and the bride steps into the room for all to see, most for the first time, in her wedding gown. There are almost always declarations of praise and admiration. This lady, whom so many know in her usual role as sister, daughter, friend, or neighbor, has been transformed into a princess for a short while and everyone wants to celebrate the change with her. Applause is very appropriate at that moment, although we never do.

Slowly she makes her way to the front, where her groom stands eagerly waiting her arrival. He gently takes her hands in his. As they stand there before God and the entire world, they now publicly declare that they are united, not only in heart and mind but now in spirit and soul and that nothing should separate them except death. It is sealed by a declaration from a representative of the local government or church. They are now one in the eyes of both God and man.

The pledge having been made and the declaration announced, they make their way back out through the doors through which they entered to begin a life together for all eternity.

Then the fun begins. As soon as the reception line has dispersed and the photo ops are over, everyone heads for the dining area or hall for the party. I love a good wedding party. You have gathered with friends, acquaintances, and family members to celebrate something wonderful. There is an air of joy. There are laughter and uplifting talk everywhere you turn. At a wedding party, there is rarely anyone who isn't in a good mood. That's part of the reason a wedding party is so much fun. No wonder we are told that in ancient Israel it was not uncommon for a wedding party to last as long as a week. No one wanted to go back to the drudgery of work when they were having so much fun.

There is also that feeling of accomplishment. You feel like a winner because someone you know has finally accomplished the process of dating, being engaged and pledging themselves to one another. The process of selecting a life mate has been completed with success. For many parents, this is a time of relief. Finally their son or daughter has found someone to spend life with other than under their wings of protection. Other parents see this as an accomplishment on their own part. They have successfully reared a young life to the point where he or she is ready to take on the challenges of adulthood. That child can be released into the world, prepared to meet it head on with the assistance of a good mate.

To add to this atmosphere of success are the food and drink. There are usually plenty of both. The centerpiece of the food table is the wedding cake. Beautifully decorated to fit the occasion, it stands in its special place of honor waiting for the newlywed couple to cut the first slice and present it to each other in a token of servitude.

It is a very rare occasion where someone leaves a wedding feast still hungry. There is usually more than enough food to feed all those who came. Apparently this has been the case for centuries, even in the Jewish culture of old. Jesus talks about a man who had prepared such a feast in his day and that many people were invited to celebrate the feast with him (Matt. 22:1–14).

Food, drink, and music are all integral parts of a good wedding celebration. Let there be plenty of food and lots to drink that all may feel merry for such an event. After all, it should be a once-in-a-lifetime celebration if it was properly thought through and planned according to God's will and advice.

Now I'm not a dancer, but for most people, there is also the celebratory first dance by the honored couple. After that, the bride usually dances with her father, if he is present, and the groom with his mother. When our youngest daughter was married, she implored me to dance with her, if even for few minutes. I tried. I really did. But I wonder if she then realized how poor a dancer I was. I didn't intend to spoil the moment for her, but I just couldn't dance. I still can't.

When the special dances are over, then everyone else joins in. By this time, the party is in full swing. Music, food, dancing and being with people you know and love. What could be better?

Somewhere in the middle of all the festivities is the opening of gifts. Again each couple handles this differently according to the plan they formulated before the ceremony. Norman and Melinda stopped dancing and partying long enough to open each gift carefully and publicly thanking each giver who was in attendance. Part of the fun was to see what they had received as love offerings from family and friends.

John and Louise did not open their gifts at the party. They had asked the best man and the bride's maid to pack them and deliver the boxes to the home, where they would live after returning from the honeymoon. Later they would open them and acknowledge each gift with a special thank-you card.

A third couple, Don and Cheryl, designated two lady friends to open the gifts for them while the party was going on and display them on a table designated for that purpose. Those ladies logged each gift and the giver. David and Cheryl would write thank-you notes after they settled in their new home together.

There was nothing wrong with any of the choices made. Each chose to handle the gifts in the way that best suited the occasion. Personalizing the wedding and the reception is what it is all about. It is their celebration; they should be able to do it the way they want and what works for them. Duane Garrett and Paul House, in their commentary on the Song of Solomon *(Word Biblical Commentary),* say, "The glory of the wedding is in the ceremony and elaborate costuming. The glory of a marriage is in the love of a man and a woman."

When any couple sets the date for their wedding, it triggers a flurry of activity. There is much to be done. In most cases, the groom and his family, at least here in America, tend to lie back and let the bride's family take care of most of the details. The bride and her mother, girlfriends, or other close relatives *must* go shopping for everything from flowers to candles, from dresses to centerpieces. The cake needs to be ordered. The person to officiate contacted, and so on.

In all of this activity, the couple needs to talk things through. Unfortunately, in many cases, this does not happen and what should be the happiest day of their lives turns out to be one that triggers fights, anger, and regrets. That is no way to start a marriage.

Steve and Deanna found themselves in such a position. By the time their wedding day arrived, Steve was steaming and Deanna was downcast. It all began when Deanna went shopping with one of her best friends who had accepted the invitation to be her maid of honor. Steve knew nothing of this. He knew Roxanne a little since she was Deanna's friend but did not really care for her because of her interfering attitude. When they returned from their shopping trip, his fears were confirmed. Because of her strong influence and ability to talk Deanna into doing things, they came back with things that were not needed or were more expensive than necessary. Steve asked who was going to pay for all of it and did not like the answer he got. Anger got the best of him, and he had to leave the house to calm down.

In the days ahead, there were more scenes similar to this, and rather than being excited about the wedding, Steve was not happy at all. Even when his future father-in-law offered to help pay for the wedding, it didn't take away Steve's feeling of being left out of the decision process. It appeared that Deanna was adamant about having the wedding *she* wanted, never mind what anyone else thought or advised.

It didn't help when Deanna approached Steve about a matter related to the wedding that he would almost always shrug his shoulders and let her do what she had in mind. He chose not to deal with the matter. He hated to confront her about anything. When he did, it felt like he was speaking out of place. Let her learn from her mistakes. If it came up later, he could say it was not anything that he did to create the problem.

Deanna's attitude was to please herself with a beautiful wedding at almost any cost. Steve's thoughts were that he just wanted to be left alone. She wanted the wedding to be focused on her. He wanted the wedding over with so he could live in peace.

Preparing for the most precious and blessed event in a couple's life should not lead to strife, anger, fear, or resentment.

Mark and Hannah approached the blessed day in a whole different way. Once they had made the commitment to each other and to God, they gradually brought up the subjects that needed to be discussed. As each topic became the center of discussion, they would try to see it from different angles or viewpoints to determine the best solution. In the end, Hannah, along with her mother, as much as she was able in spite of dealing with her terminal cancer, and girlfriends were given the responsibility of planning the decorations and the selection of who would wear what. Mark did participate in the selection of the color theme. He and Hannah talked it through and decided on lavender and white. The details he left to the ladies.

Mark, having already set the date with Hannah and in discussion with their respective families, was to choose the time, place, and who would officiate. He would also select his male wedding partners to stand up with him. He and his Dad, now recovered somewhat from his stroke, would oversee the work of arranging tables, hiring the music, choosing a caterer, and other things not delegated to the women.

As each of them came to a decision, it was not hidden or kept secret. Both Mark and Hannah shared with the other what had been accomplished and asked advice on matters still to be done. From the time of their engagement, they had allowed more than a year to give themselves plenty of time to make good decisions and for Hannah to finish her college education. Mark would still have a few more years of study, but she would be finished and could become employed to help with household and school expenses. Not being rushed made a wonderful and shared experience they both enjoyed and remembered for a long, long time. Because Mark allowed Hannah the freedom to be herself and to plan according to her wishes, she felt no remorse or guilt and since Hannah did not try to impose her ideas on Mark and his male friends the entire process went very well. They saw this as a mutual commitment which demanded mutual respect and sharing. There was no "living for me" involved.

Any intimate relationship should be based on what we can give, not what we can get. This is especially true of a marriage, which is intended to be a union for life with the intent of producing, with God's blessing, offspring that can be taught how to live meaningful lives.

When we read in scripture what is taught about marriage and family relationships, we never find advice that is self-centered. It is always focused on the others in the family. The husband is to love, cherish, and care for his wife. The wife is to show respect and concern for him and to encourage her husband in his endeavors. The children should be brought up to show kindness, respect, and obedience to their parents, and the parents are to treat their children as valuable young people who have a measure of worth and importance, not only in the family but in society. See Ephesians 5:22–6:4.

You want a marriage that fulfills you and meets your needs?

Be a man who tries to meet the needs of your wife. Become the wife who puts the needs and desires of her husband above her own. Learn to show mutual respect for each other, even when the other person disappoints you or upsets you. Always keep in mind that God has brought you together for the purpose of building up the other, not to give you satisfaction or have your selfish desires met.

Pause and Reflect

Describe the most beautiful wedding you have witnessed. What made it so wonderful?

Have you ever questioned the union of two people you knew were intent on getting married? What made you wonder if it was a good idea?

Among your friends, whose wedding went the smoothest in the planning? Whose went all wrong? Why?

Have you witnessed a situation where one or the other (or their parents) took command of the planning and did not listen to other people's advice or attempts to help? What was the result?

Have you ever witnessed that on their wedding day some people looked like they wished they were somewhere else?

If you have been married, describe the planning process. Was it done jointly with your spouse, or was it a one-sided effort?

Did things go smoothly? Was there a lot of stress and headache? How were decisions made?

Looking back, would you have done things differently?

After You're Wed: Facing Life's Challenges Together

Trust

A good marriage is based in mutual trust. He must be able to trust her with responsibilities, decisions, and relationships outside the marriage. She needs to trust him in the same way and for the same reasons: doubts and suspicions are wedges that can cause severe cracks in their union.

From the other side of this argument is the fact that a good spouse does not do things that cause doubt or suspicion. A man will prove himself dependable, reliable, and considerate toward his wife. A woman will do her part to support him by carrying enough of the load of responsibility that he will not feel overly burdened and worn out. She too will show how dependable she can be, and her decisions would prove that she cares more about the relationship than her personal desires. These things can be done in a variety of ways.

Lawrence and Cindy had all the visions of young couples. They wanted life to be easy, productive, and enjoyable for them both. Soon after they were married, Lawrence realized how hard Cindy worked to keep up with the housework, go to work, and maintain the schedule of events and appointments they had on their calendar. Because he often arrived home first, he developed the habit of starting dinner before she got home. Many times he would notice that she had gotten behind with the laundry, so he would put a load in the washer or the dryer as needed. He found that it was not difficult to give the kitchen floor a quick sweep or to simply load the dishwasher with the dishes that had been left as they rushed out the door to their respective places of employment.

For her part, Cindy learned that Lawrence didn't always have the time to keep the lawn mowed or the flowers and bushes tended to. On weekends or evenings that she was not committed to other things, she would do whatever she could to help him in that regard. It took her only a few minutes to sweep the porch, to weed the flowers, or to trim the hedge. She knew they were things that did not need to be left for Lawrence to do when he could. Because she wanted to be of help to him and to show some pride in their property, she was willing to pitch in when and however she could.

A good marriage partner will not be jealous, suspicious, or threatened by relationships outside the marriage. Many marriages are broken up by unnecessary jealousy or suspicion of infidelity. A committed spouse will not do anything or say anything that will arouse such feelings. He or she will be very careful to live above suspicion by avoiding times alone with individuals the spouse may have reason to be jealous of. When one of them leaves to go somewhere without the spouse, there should be enough trust and respect to allow that person to go without wondering how the other person will react. There should be enough trust to make the one who goes out to be at peace that all will be well when they arrive home and not be subjected to an interrogation.

He should have enough faith in her to let her spend time with her lady friends, and she should respect his time away from her doing things that he likes without her tagging along. There are things that they should enjoy together, and there are things that each of them could enjoy while apart. To do those things knowing the other one is supportive and encouraging brings a great deal of peace to the individual as well as to the marriage union.

When Betsy and Brian were married, they had to work through such trust issues. Whenever Brian went out somewhere without Betsy, she would insist on knowing where he went and who he was with. As soon as Brian realized what was going on, he had a frank talk with Betsy about trust. They discussed the relationship between love and trust, including how truly loving someone lets you trust that person to make decisions, to be faithful, and to act responsibly. They also talked about how insisting on knowing every detail of the other's activities is a control issue that needs to be resolved. After about an hour of honest dialogue, Betsy realized what she was doing was not good, apologized to Brian, and vowed to try hard not to do those things. After that, things improved greatly for them.

In the relationship between Mark and Hannah, the issue was not so much a matter of distrust in loyalty as it was in responsibility. Mark really loved his family very much but sometimes just got so distracted by his work and other activities that he would forget to pick up a child from practice or to bring them home from the sitter's after work. More than once he would arrive home believing he would relax a while before dinner only to have Hannah ask, "Where are the kids?" He then would sheepishly have to admit that he forgot he was supposed to bring them home with him. Or at other times he would be about to leave work when a colleague would engage him in conversation about something and time would get away from them. First thing he knows, there is a signal from his phone, and he realizes it's someone from the school wondering where he is. His neglect to pay attention to this matter got to the point where it was costing them time and money for him to have to retrace his steps to retrieve the child or children, let alone causing him embarrassment every time.

Finally, Hannah had enough and got him a new phone that included an appointment feature so he could put into it the times and dates he had to be there for his kids. Trust is not always about loyalty. Sometimes it is about responsibility. Mark had to learn to be more responsible in the matter of dealing with coordinating his schedule with those of his family members. It took a while and some practice, but he got much better at it and relished the times when he could be at home and not have to say he forgot one of them.

No matter how strong the union is, no matter how much support and encouragement you show, no matter how much you say you love your spouse, there will be times when you just honestly disagree and you think he is the most pigheaded and stubborn man alive. You may be convinced that she is the most uncaring and selfish person you have ever met. Those times go with the territory of marriage. Fortunately, in a good marriage, those times are brief and infrequent because the individuals within the marriage will not let those childish thoughts become fighting words. At some point, they become mature enough to realize the damage it can cause to allow such petty thoughts to come between them. Then they confess their wrong and hurtful thoughts, words, and acts, ask forgiveness, and move on. A good marriage is founded on mutual trust, respect, and encouragement. When those things are in place, there is not much that can shake the bond between them.

Life may not be the smooth path to success they envision as young adults, but it can be enjoyable as long as they live together on this earth.

Pause and Reflect

If you are in a relationship, look at the other person and ask yourself, "Do I trust him or her with every aspect of our relationship?"

Are there areas where I have been disappointed because the other person did not hold up to my expectations?

Do I get jealous, even a little, when my significant other spends time away from me with other people?

Have we had heated discussions about money? Chores? Responsibilities in or outside the home?

On a scale of 1 to 10, with 1 being "no trust at all" and 10 being "a complete trust," where would you put your level of trust in your spouse or potential spouse?

If your answer is below a 7, perhaps you should reconsider your relationship or get help learning to trust.

Careers

People say money and sex are the two biggest issues that divide couples. I would add that career choices would rank up there equal to or even higher than one of those. When they get together, both partners usually have already been settled into a career right out of high school or college. Over and over again, we hear the mantra that we should pursue our personal goals in life and let nothing stop us. That sounds fine but doesn't work when two people who love each other are trying to make their relationship work. If we are to be united as a single unit as God says we should see ourselves, individuality is foregone for the sake of the union. That career or vocation we have learned to do so well may have to be sacrificed.

Our modern culture has conditioned us to believe that it is necessary for both parties to be in the workforce to be able to afford the good things in life we deserve. That may or may not be true. But nevertheless, it is a statistical fact that it is very rare for a couple to try to live on one income. So how do we work out a solution to make marriage work when we spend the majority of our time at work, not with our spouses? Unfortunately some cling to their career as if their very lives depend on it instead of looking at other options to honor the pledge made at the wedding ceremony to provide and care for the other person. We all know someone who was or became a workaholic, trying to advance in his or her company and make a name for himself or herself. That focus on the career drowns out all cries for attention from the spouse who is left behind.

Consider what happened to Glenn and Stacey. When they were married, Glenn worked for an insurance company as a claims adjuster. Stacey was a manager for a large department store. Both of them had a few years of experience and were rooted in place careerwise. Glenn had his eye on becoming the head of the agency where he worked. He not only did his job well but spent a lot of time studying other aspects of the insurance industry so he would be in a position to advance as soon as a higher position opened up. As an adjuster, he would often go out to visit places that had claims filed to be sure there was no hint of fraud or deception. Although he tried to keep his hours reasonable, there were times when he would be gone overnight or for a day or two. Stacey didn't like that but made the best of it.

For her own part, Stacey worked irregular hours and could not be depended on to be there when Glenn got home in the evening. It was hard for him to keep up with his wife's schedule because it was always changing. In addition to her scheduled shift, Stacey often volunteered to cover for an absent employee or worked extra hours during rush times or in holiday shopping periods. When she was home, she was so exhausted she did not feel like doing much. The house was untidy, and the two of them rarely spent quality time together. This was one of Glenn's pet peeves and the source of many arguments.

In this household, there were two individuals passing by each other occasionally, two people focused on pleasing themselves. They both enjoyed their work and didn't mind the extra effort needed to advance in their respective companies. What they soon realized was that their marriage was suffering terribly. Stacey, being the more sensitive one, was scared. She was scared because Glenn did not appreciate her not being a better housekeeper or not always being there for him when he needed her. She was scared that in desperation he might find someone who would better serve his personal needs or desires. She was scared that this marriage just might dissolve since the two of them were not really united on the matter of careers. Glenn was more matter-of-fact about the situation. As he understood it, if Stacey stayed with him, that was the best thing, but if she wanted out, he would not stop her because he understood the drive that fueled her ambitions at the store. Either way, he would survive.

After four years of living this farce of a marriage, pretending everything was all right, they decided it would be better to go their separate ways.

Allen and Marcie also had separate careers. He was a loan officer in a bank. She worked nights in a factory on an assembly line. Allen would get up in the morning and be at work by eight. Marcie would come home at midnight and sleep until nine or ten. While Allen was at work providing money for other people to meet their financial needs, Marcie was home enjoying the time alone to do household chores, go shopping, or whatever came to mind that day. She was free to spend time doing things that were either necessary or fun. By three o'clock, she was back at work and Allen was preparing to come home to an empty house. Only when one or both of them had a day off did they get to spend any time together. Even then they did not usually do anything together but focused on the chores around the house.

On Sunday they would attend church, and everyone would remark how well adjusted they seemed to be. What did not show on the surface was the trouble that was brewing underneath. Both of them hated the thought of not spending much time with each other but were locked into their jobs by credit card debt or unpaid bills. Each felt that their income was necessary to keep up with the expenses. So they plugged along.

What they were slowly beginning to see was the damage the situation was inflicting on their marriage. Allen was beginning to feel neglected. He resented, not a little bit, the apparent freedom Marcie had to do things while he was at work but he couldn't do because by the time he got home and had dinner, there was less activity going on in the community. Marcie as well was feeling lonely. Waking up each morning and finding the house empty and still empty when she left for work made her life less enjoyable than she wanted.

One day they had a frank talk about the situation. Allen made it clear that he would not leave his position at the bank. Not only did it provide them with a good income, but he felt he was providing a much-needed service to the community. He thought it would work if Marcie quit her job at the factory. Marcie put her foot down. The income she received from her job, even though it did not pay very well, was enough for her to save for special occasions or to buy those little extras they appreciated around the house like a new chair or appliances. She wondered how they would pay the bills if she did not have her paycheck to contribute to them.

Allen argued that if she didn't have the income to depend on, perhaps she wouldn't spend so much in the first place. They argued back and forth for one whole afternoon. They never did resolve the matter to the satisfaction of either of them. Actually it made matters worse because now they both resented the other's point of view. Any resemblance of peace and accord was gone.

Mark and Hannah approached the matter of separate careers early on in their relationship. They both understood the passion each had for serving people through medicine. They also realized that it would be very easy to get pulled in different directions by opportunity to advance or pursue paths that would take apart. Knowing that it is God's will that they honor their vows to protect, respect, and uphold each other, they committed themselves to following only those opportunities that would not interfere with their relationship.

Even before graduation, Mark was offered a position in a major hospital, but to take that job, he would have to move and work long and unpredictable hours. That would have put an unreasonable strain on Hannah by leaving her alone much of the time, and if the Lord should bless them with children, Mark would miss out on much of their nurturing. Had he been living selfishly, Mark could have received a position of esteem, a measure of wealth, and good standing in the community, but it would have put a severe strain on the relationship with the woman he loved and believed God had brought into his life. Mark's choice was to work in and eventually operate a small clinic near his hometown and be able to be home as much as possible.

Hannah had to wrestle with the decision of working or staying home. After their first child was born, it became a juggling feat to fit the needs of the child, and later other children, into a two-income lifestyle. The solution for her was to simply cut back on the hours she worked at the clinic meeting other children's needs medically and concentrate on her own.

The solution Mark and Hannah worked out was one of giving up selfish desires for the sake of their marriage and family. For them it was not really a sacrifice but a joyful giving up of personal goals to experience the wonderful life of a close family. When each new opportunity for career change or advancement came along, they prayed together and made a decision they knew God would be pleased with and would benefit them as a couple, not one individual over the other.

In today's world, it is very difficult to live on one income. The decision is not really whether or not both of you will work but if you will let your career interfere with your relationship to your spouse. However you work it out, God will honor that decision as long as you honor him in it, and one of the best ways to honor him is to hold your marriage vows dear and sacred.

Pause and Reflect

There are still people who insist that the woman's place is in the home. Is this realistic in today's economic climate? Why or why not?

Have you and the person you are in a relationship with discussed your separate careers?

Are either of you in a career that could potentially pull you away?

When a new position is offered to you, how much time will you spend in prayer before you make the decision to accept or pass?

Does your spouse's current employment offer opportunities to advance?

How would you feel if he or she was offered a position that would take him or her to another city?

How would such an offer affect your own employment?

Since God expects the husband to provide for and meet the needs of his wife and family, making major decisions (Ephesians 5:22–33), what process would benefit both of you? At what level should you be involved in the decision?

Handling Money

Money, we are told, is the root of all evil. It certainly can be the cause of much marital strife. Too many times the individuals see their income as "my money" and "her money." So when the paycheck comes in, the guy will often use it to buy something, do something, or go somewhere because it pleases him. What is left over he will put into the joint account to pay the bills. But men are not entirely the ones to blame in this practice. Women have the same impulses. They believe that if they earn money, they have the right and privilege of spending it, especially if they want to use it to indulge a child, grandchild, or themselves.

Some people are very responsible and wise in how they handle money. Others are careless and cannot be trusted with the bank accounts. In any marriage, there needs to be at least one who is capable of keeping the family books up to date and balanced. That person should be the designated money handler.

Pat made it clear from the beginning that she wanted to help with the family finances, so she and Richard initiated the habit of sitting down every few days to discuss what needed to be paid and what financial plans they wanted to make for their future. They learned to trust each other to follow through on the decisions they made. When one of them wanted to spend money on something that had not been discussed, the other would remind them of the goals they had set and how this new expense would affect those goals. They trusted each other enough to make good decisions but also depended on each other to help keep one another in line with the decisions they had made.

Living frugally does not necessarily mean going without. It does mean making choices on what to buy and when to make those purchases. Many books have been written, and there are online blogs that are very helpful to guide a person or couple with learning to spend wisely instead of impulsively. Money is easily wasted on expensive products and services that can be purchased for less and not sacrifice quality. Part of living within your budget is learning to seek out those bargains that fit your family's needs in a timely way. Watching for sales (real sales, not discounted inflated prices), buying in the off season, or taking advantage of store closings are some of the ways to save. But be careful! Buying just because it's on sale is not a bargain if it's something you may never use.

My wife and I knew of a couple many years ago that were very immature in dealing with finances. First of all, they did not have much income, and that was irregular. When one of them received a paycheck from a job, they were both quick to splurge like the money would last forever. The bills did not get paid on time. The cupboards did not contain much food, and the car was always in need of repair. Neither of them took responsibility for the funds God had allowed them to have. They ended up very unhappy and finally divorced.

In the matter of money, there needs to be one partner who can be expected to keep things under control, even if we don't like the penny-pinching necessary. I very rarely have much cash in my wallet for two reasons. First, I don't trust myself to spend it wisely. I am always tempted to buy on impulse if I have the money in my pocket. The second reason is that I have learned that the money that I would use for selfish pleasures (a candy bar, ice cream, a book I shouldn't read in the first place, etc.) could be used to pay down a debt. Together my wife and I understand that it is better to forego temporary pleasure to meet long-term goals. She trusts me to not overspend when I go to the store, and I trust her to keep the books and pay the bills.

The Bible has a lot to say about money beyond the warning

that it can lead to trouble. It shows us that all we have comes from the hand of God, and God expects us to handle it wisely, invest in the future, and plan to leave a small nest egg for our offspring, all while we learn to be generous while we live. In one illustration, Jesus rebukes the kind of person who would hoard money thinking he would be safe to do so. Thinking in selfish terms relating to money is not in God's plan.

Giving is a wonderful way to support a cause or a ministry. But as the scriptures teach us, it is the motive behind the giving that is most important (2 Corinthians 9:6–7).

Jeff and Kate were faithful worshipers at their local church. They rarely missed attendance at Sunday services and often also were found at the other times of Bible study. Both of them had been Christians for a long time and had reared their children to love and serve the Lord as well. By all accounts, they were typical churchgoers.

One of the topics that their pastor often emphasized was generous giving to the Lord's ministry. He would point out Bible verses that talked about tithing or having a positive attitude when we contribute a portion of financial income back to God. Over and over again, they heard messages about the subject. But like most who worship the Lord, they had their own ideas on how much they should give, and the two of them could not come to a real agreement on the subject.

Jeff was more in favor of writing a check for a fixed amount every week so it could be budgeted more easily. He didn't really care about how big the check was as long as it varied very little in size. Sometimes he would say to Kate, "There are plenty of other people in the church besides us. We are not responsible to meet the entire need. Besides, I know there are some who make a lot more money than we do. If they paid their tithe, there wouldn't be much need for the rest of us to do that."

Kate's usual response was that having that kind of attitude didn't relieve them from their duty as Christians to give proportionally or generously. She was more in favor of donating what was left over after the bills were paid and there was enough in the bank to meet their short-term plans. This would mean the amount would vary, but they would not be locked into a giving plan or any fixed amount. She took the statement "God loves a cheerful giver" literally. She understood that to write a check that would be given at the cost of foregoing a bill or a personal purchase would be given grudgingly, not with cheer.

What was unusual about their giving habits is not that they could not agree on the methodology and the amount but that it was inconsistent with what they each gave as the reason for their point of view. For instance, Kate wanted to only give what they could "afford" at the end of each pay period. Yet she thought nothing about committing a fixed amount to be given to her favorite nonprofit charity. Each time they send an appeal letter, she dutifully would contribute the same amount. To her, it was a simple matter of checking a box on the response card, filling out her credit card information, and popping it in the mail. There were no thoughts about giving leftovers or searching her wallet to see how much she could afford to give.

Jeff, being the methodical and consistent one, would also occasionally give to charities outside of the church. To him, when a worthy cause presented itself (and he was very selective), he would consider it carefully and give a one-time donation. He did not commit himself or the family budget to constant pleas for funds. For Jeff, it was more a spur-of-the-moment decision than planned giving, which was just the opposite of what he insisted they do when giving to the Lord's work.

Jeff and Kate never really worked out a mutual plan to be more consistent or more biblical in the way they donated their money. At times it became a sore spot between them because each wanted the funds to be handled the way they felt was right. Neither would give in to the idea that there may be a better way. Neither of them was open to discussion about why they had these differences of opinion. So the tension remained, and the friction wore at them day after day, week after week, year after year with no change. Both Jeff and Kate were "living for me" in the sense that what each of them determined was the right method should be the one that was followed. My opinion is the better one, so let's follow it. The problem was that as long as they couldn't agree, there was little joy in their giving.

Mark and Hannah had long been acquainted with the biblical

mandates relating to giving an offering to the Lord of their income. Since both of them were on salary, it was not difficult to determine a percentage they were both content with.

They both had been exposed to the teaching of a tithe, giving 10 percent to the Lord. They both had also heard a lot of sermons on giving cheerfully, not grudgingly or under compulsion. For them, the matter was not a question of how much or how often as a duty but how much they love the Lord. As Mark put it once when the subject came up early in their relationship, "If it was a thank-you gift to another person for something special they had done, how much would we offer?" In other words, how thankful are we for all the wonderful things God has done? So they set a minimum of 10 percent, but as they paid off a bill or received a generous bonus or raise, they would increase the amount a little. After a period of several years, the percentage had increased considerably, but they did not hesitate to write the checks. It was a joy to give so others might know this same God they serve. There was no comparing of themselves with anyone else. It was a matter between them and God. The method did not require any thought or debate. It was simple math put into practice at the beginning of each pay period. God received his token gift, and then the bill collectors each got their share. For Mark and Hannah, giving was a privilege, not an obligation.

Unfortunately, there are way too many people who think of themselves first when it comes to money. What can I do with my paycheck this week? How much will be left for me to use after I pay the bills? If I buy this boat, this camper, this new television or whatever, can I still keep the bill collectors away? If I have a choice between buying something for pleasure and giving money away, I rather spend it on myself. "Living for me" does not take sharing with others or giving back to the Lord in high regard. The result is that they are never really satisfied. The hunger to meet selfish desires is never filled. But if a person develops a generous spirit, sharing his income with others in need and giving back to the Lord a portion of his material blessings, there is a deep sense of satisfaction of knowing you have invested in someone other than yourself (Proverbs 3:27–28).

There is much to be said on this topic, but the point is that even with our money, we should learn not to be self-centered. We should use it for the benefit of our family welfare, for those in need, and to honor God who gave it to us, not necessarily in that order. Couples and families have been broken up way too often because one or both of the partners tried to use money to satisfy himself or herself.

Money can bring heartache and strife, or it can bring unity and happiness. Being unselfish brings much greater joy than being stingy and tight or to spend money recklessly.

Pause and Reflect

Who is responsible for paying the bills in your household?

How did you come to that conclusion?

Is the other person capable of handling finances in a responsible way? Is he or she willing to learn?

When was the last time you spent a large sum on a purchase for yourself without consulting your spouse or fiancé?

Have the two of you ever argued over an expense one of you thought was unnecessary or untimely? How was the situation resolved?

Have you ever sacrificed a selfish pleasure to meet a financial obligation? How did you feel?

Do you believe it is wise to take on a second (or third) job to meet the expenses of large purchases, such as camper, boat, and motorcycle?

If you worship regularly, do you and your spouse have a plan for how much you give back to God?

When it comes to giving to charities or nonprofits, do you have an agreed-on plan, or do you give spontaneously?

Does your budget include saving for the future, or will you let the future take care of itself?

Have you discussed your children's educational financing for college or university?

Where Do We Live?

R esidency can be a complex issue, or it can be a very simple one. Where will we live after we become husband and wife? Many factors can make the decision difficult, including proximity to work or school, distance from family, and the size of the house. How much of our income can we afford to put into rent or a mortgage? Will the place need a lot of repair and maintenance or is it relatively new and only needs upkeep?

For many couples, the question of where they will live has already been worked out well ahead of time, but for others, it has not. Every couple has to deal with the decision relating to residency. Often one or the other will simply move in with the new spouse and share one space rather than live apart as they did before. Other couples go through the agonizing process of deciding what is best for them, given their unique set of circumstances. But no matter how it works, there is a decision that has to be made.

Dean and Valerie were planning their wedding for early June after he graduated college. Valerie came from a well-established family in her community, and the house where she had called home for most of her life was available. Her parents had moved into a retirement center and no longer needed it. If she and Dean did not wish to live there, it would go on the market. Her heart was set on keeping the property in the family and raising her own children in the same house she had grown up in.

Dean's family had been poor when he grew up and had no property to speak of. His new office where he had found employment was fifty miles away in another town, making a long commute each way every day. He had no attachment to any one place and favored moving closer to his work. He was sure they could find a good house and good schools for any children they might have. For him, there were no deep roots anywhere.

They could each be stubborn. Valerie argued that her former home would cost very little and give them a sense of stability and heritage for their children. Because of her deep attachments to the community, she was nervous about moving to a new place and having to force herself to make new friends. Dean, on the other hand, argued that being close to work would mean he could spend more time with the family and fewer expenses related to travel. He added that a newer home might be less expensive in the long run because an older house would require more upkeep and maintenance. He also told Valerie that her fears about moving were childish and unfounded, which didn't help. The arguments were frequent and furious; neither wanted to give in to the other.

Dean finally convinced Valerie to at least go look at a house he had his eye on. It was located halfway between her old residence and his work. When she saw it and the potential it had for them as well as the long-term financial gain they would receive, she agreed to move. But it was with a sense of loss and fear for the future that she packed up the old house to move into the new one. There was no real joy in it for her.

This could, alternatively, be a chance to show unselfish love as it was for Mark and Hannah. Knowing her strong attachment to her former home and her parents, Mark talked with Hannah about the pros and cons of living in her old home, at least temporarily. He was more than willing to find a position at an area clinic, even if he had to drive several miles to be there since he knew it would make her happy to be near her ailing mother and in a familiar environment. For Mark, the goal was not to do well financially as a result of his training but to meet the needs of his patients and their families. His student loan debt would take care of itself over time as long as they learned to live within their means. So he was perfectly contented to please Hannah in the matter of where they lived.

Hannah, for her part, could see Mark's need for moving closer to a clinic that would pay him well and offer other benefits, detaching her from past roots and moving out on their own. She understood that her mother needed medical attention beyond Hannah's capabilities and even that of Mark. But staying near her parents would not have any greater benefit than the weekly visits she was already making. They could stay in touch by phone or email during the week. The house itself had no special attachments for Hannah. Although she grew up in it and loved every part of it, she realized the enormous task it would be to keep it up. It had been built in the early sixties with structural features and wiring and plumbing that certainly did not meet modern codes. Though it was livable, it wasn't ideal and she would have no regrets leaving it behind. If Mark found a good home nearer a clinic that promised him plenty of work and good pay, she would have no hesitation to move there.

If any couple followed the biblical principle for marriage, they would calmly discuss the matter and commit it to prayer, asking God's guidance. When the time came to make up their minds, Mark should take the lead and commit to one or the other, taking into consideration all the information they had and respecting Hannah's feelings. Whichever way he chose, it would be a decision they both could live with. He would know that they made the best decision for their future and she would respect his decision as the head of their home, trusting his judgment. He would do what he thought best because he loved her, and she would follow his leadership because she loved him enough to accept his decision, even if she didn't agree 100 percent with it.

In the end, Mark chose to stay put in Hannah's old house because not only would they both have student loan debt, but he would be required to spend at least a year in residency at a nearby hospital. So for the next two years at least, they were not ready to commit to the financial, emotional, and physical drain a move would entail. Sharing the home with her parents would be a blessing for them as well as provide comfort and care for Hannah's parents with the death of her mother seemingly only a short time away.

"Living for me" would insist that each of them puts their respective feet down and demands the other to see things differently. It would cause fights, hurt feelings, and emotional trauma. There would be plenty of excitement between them, but it would be almost all fireworks rather than the warm glow of friendship and love. In the end, "living for me" is divisive and destructive. A good marriage should be such that the couple draw closer to each other rather than be driven apart.

Pause and Reflect

For the unmarried:

Do you have a preference about where you will live after the ceremony?

Have you and your potential mate discussed this matter at length?

Was it an easy decision?

What was the deciding factor on where you will live?

For the married:

What was the first house you lived in as a couple like?

Have you moved since?

What were the circumstances that caused a move?

Did you both participate equally in the process? If not, why not?

Are you happy with where you are living now?

How does (did) your relationship with God influence your decision?

Children

That child who is always getting on your nerves is a gift from God, so we're told. It does not always seem to be true. Children who misbehave regularly have emotional or physical handicaps or just seem to drain all the energy out of their parents surely don't make the gift very welcome. Many parents or parents-to-be feel burdened by the responsibility that comes with having children. That is why there is a public debate on how many children a couple should have and be responsible parents.

This may seem like a private and very personal matter, but believe me: it has become a loud and long public issue. A couple of generations ago, there was little or no debate over this because there was no ready access to treatments or clinics that could be used to limit reproduction. Every family had a houseful of kids simply because there was no way to stop them from arriving other than to refrain from the act that produced them. It was not uncommon for homes to have eight or more children. Some families I am familiar with had eleven or twelve. One even had nineteen!

Now, however, with thoughts of careers pushing aside family life, the readily available resources, and the freedom that comes by not having many children, almost every couple comes to the point where they begin to think about limiting their family size. This was something my wife and I faced. It was an easy decision for me, but Linda struggled with it for a long time, both before and after the decision that three children were enough.

Many women tend to let the maternal instinct govern their thoughts on this matter. They love children and the more, the better. If God blessed them with only one or with twenty-one, they would accept it from the hand of God. We are told that even from the earliest days, women did not feel fulfilled if they did not have a child or children to hold in their arms and to train as they grew up. Some women still feel that way. But in today's world, there are other motivating factors that play into the equation that couples of the past did not have to face.

Victor and Rachel have been married now for almost five years. Victor works at a local factory and earns an average wage. Rachel had worked part time until her second child came along. Now she stays home to be with the children because to hire daycare for the two of them would cost more than she was earning. They were barely staying ahead of the monthly bills and still owed a large sum to the hospital. Victor was concerned that having more children would put them further into debt and overcrowd their already tight living quarters. More children would create more headaches and possibly more heartaches as well. He urged Rachel to consider not having any more.

Rachel was the motherly type and enjoyed her time with the children and even had, with Victor's permission, opened up her home to watch the children of another family that was struggling. Her attitude was "the more the merrier." She had convinced herself that she would have as many as God allowed naturally. She felt it an offense to God to try to prevent future pregnancies.

How would they handle this big decision? Would they argue and fight now about this and continue to argue and fight later when other issues come up relating to this, blaming each other for the outcome? Victor could insist that she have the necessary surgery or go on birth control pills. He could go to the doctor himself without Rachel's consent and have the necessary surgery to stop with two children. If Victor insisted on having his own way, there would be no more, beginning right now.

Rachel would be helpless to stop him from having surgery, but if he chose not to, there were ways she could get her own way.

Surgery could be refused, pills could be skipped once in a while, or she could simply not do anything and let nature take its course. Victor would have to somehow live with any more children they might have.

Since Victor wanted no more children and Rachel did, there was a conflict that had to be resolved. If they both insisted on trying to get their own way, there would always be hard feelings and resentment. One or the other at some point would have to concede to the will of their spouse, though it would not be easy nor would it make them love and respect each other more. Rather, it would remain as wedge between them for as long as the hurt feelings remained. "Living for me" becomes a weapon of discord and division in a home that desires peace and unity.

Rob loved children. He told his wife Jan that he would hope they had a houseful. Jan, for her part, was skeptical about having any more than the three they already had. Not only were they keeping her busy, the constant activity taxed her energy almost to the point of collapse. Every night she went to bed dreading the thought of doing it all again the next day.

When she approached Rob about limiting their family size, he was disappointed. He thought she was just being selfish about the matter. Even after Jan pointed out how tired she was each night, he still thought it was just a way of her getting what she wanted. She could be so manipulative sometimes. They heatedly discussed the subject often for more than a month until Jan finally told him that she was going to the doctor and get it taken care of. That made Rob furious.

Not only did he not go with her to the clinic for the operation, when she came home he was nowhere to be found. He had left the three children with their maternal grandparents and simply disappeared. Jan did not hear from him for almost six weeks. He did not report for work; he did not call or write; he did not communicate at all. Finally, she got a note in the mail saying he was filing for a divorce because they did not seem to be compatible any longer. "Living for me" broke up what started out to be a happy home. Now neither of them succeeded in getting what they wanted. Rob could no longer be a father to the children he already had, let alone more of them, and Jan had lost a good home and family to function in. Life can be so cruel when we live for ourselves.

Mark truly loves Hannah. Because he loves her, he would consider her desire to have children seriously. He understood that to bring more than two children into their family would create hardships for them both. For him, it meant extra mouths to feed and bodies to clothe as well as the necessary investment in their lives that children require. He was very aware that his duties to the clinic and hospital would be disruptive to his family life, and if Hannah also fulfilled her dream to become a pediatric nurse, she too would be committed to her work on an on-call basis.

Mark would not viciously and neglectfully override her feelings to get his own way. He knew that any decision they made had to be one they both would agree to and live with.

As his wife and mother of two beautiful children, Hannah in her love for Mark considered the financial commitment, the hardships more children would create, and the increase of her own workload. Now that they had settled down into some sort of routine, if you could call a doctor's life settled, Hannah could see what more children would do to their lives. There would be increased responsibilities at home with no letup of those at work. There would be times when she or Mark (or both) would have to choose between being there for their children and focusing on their patients. Adding more children would only increase the opportunities for these types of scheduling clashes. She wanted to make Mark happy whether they had two children or added one or two more. Her desire, as the Bible says, should be for her husband, not just to please him sexually but to please him all matters of life.

Hannah understood that having more children could be either a rich blessing or turn out to be a curse if the two of them were unable to meet the needs of those God had entrusted to them.

In this situation, Hannah, after much prayer and soul searching, chose to end her ability to bring more children into the world. Mark prayed with her about this, knowing how much it meant for her, and they both rejoiced that God had given them the wisdom to make a decision they believed was the right one for all concerned. There was no bitterness, no regrets, and no looking back thinking, *What if?*

A loving couple wrestling with this kind of decision should carefully and prayerfully seek God's will and place their family, both present and future into His hands. Many Christian couples have determined that having only a few children is the better choice. Others leave it totally up to God and make it work somehow with a houseful. As long as the decision is made out of love and respect for each other, then it is the right one for that couple.

Pause and Reflect

How many children do you believe is a reasonable number?

In light of God's command to the first humans to "go forth and multiply," do we have a right to prevent pregnancies?

We are told in scripture that "children are a blessing from God" and "blessed is the man who has a lot of them." Should this thought be a good reason to let nature take its course?

If you know anyone who has taken the step to prevent future children, who made the decision: the male or the female?

Has anyone you know ever expressed regret for stopping pregnancies? Why did they feel this way? Do you believe their regret is selfishly motivated?

What are some valid reasons for preventing future pregnancies?

What attitude should we express toward those who have multiple children? If they are the product of a society-dependent couple, does it affect your feelings toward them or their parent(s)?

If a couple never has any children, is that a curse or a blessing?

Are you thinking ahead about the number of children you want, or will you wait to decide that later under different circumstances?

Personal Hobbies
or Pursuits

When does a hobby become an infatuation?

Bill loved his work as a mechanic. Growing up, he had developed a passion for cars. He just enjoyed talking to other guys about them, studying all he can about them, and now as an adult working on them day and night. He couldn't seem to get his fill of motor vehicles. The auto dealership he worked at is busy, so he got to repair all kinds of vehicles. All makes and models are represented by their clients. It was an ideal job for him.

Even when he was home, Bill would tinker. He always had two or three trucks, four-wheelers, or some other vehicle sitting in the yard waiting for him to finish some project. There was always the promise that one of them would be the ticket to a dream vacation somewhere, but it never happened. One job done for a friend turned into another, and the money received for repairing one vehicle somehow got reinvested. There was no end to it.

Bill was addicted to working on motors. Many times he would work into the middle of the night to help a friend get a car ready for racing or to just help a neighbor out.

His wife did not get to see much of him and the children even less, but that was okay with Bill because he was doing what he loved to do. No amount of whining, cajoling, or pleading would keep him from getting his hands greasy. Some days he just wished Barbara would stop badgering him and let him alone. Whenever he got angry at her for bugging him, he would hide out in the garage at home and do the very thing she was asking him to set aside to spend time with her and the children. He couldn't see how much this hurt her.

When she was younger, his wife, Barbara, loved to hang around racers and hot-rodders. She liked the sound of roaring engines and the bravado of the men as they bragged up their machines and as they pitted one against another in off track or off-road competitions. It was an exciting time in her life.

Now, having been married to Bill for several years, she has matured into a woman with responsibilities, both at home and at work. They have three children she is trying to raise plus a job that requires her to be out of the home at least three days a week. It is part time, but she thought it was necessary to help meet the ever-growing expenses of keeping the home and meeting the needs of her family. Because of Bill's commitment to his job and to his tinkering when not at work, she hardly ever gets to see him except when he is sick or (rarely) takes a day off.

These are two people living in the same house with two different views on the role of a hobby. Bill works on motors because it is what he loves to do, even if it doesn't pay much or at all. He is hooked on fixing cars. Barbara sees his infatuation with engines as competition for her attention.

Couples like Bill and Barbara are all too common. We see them everywhere. Unfortunately, marriages like this are very fragile. Because of Bill's neglect, the door is wide open for Barbara to have an affair. She needs companionship and someone to show her she is appreciated. Her personal needs are being neglected for the sake of Bill's satisfaction. On the other hand, Barbara's nagging is inserting a wedge between them that could potentially drive Bill away. There are other women who hang around the rodders who might appreciate his love for cars. A younger woman just might catch his eye and offer him encouragement instead of disapproval. It would only take one innocent flirtation on either part to set off an explosion. Living with different attitudes toward hobbies can lead to disaster. "Living for me" can cause much harm to others who are part of our lives.

Bill could continue on his stubborn way and possibly lose his family. Barbara could continue to nag and whine and live with an unhappy husband and children who grow up with negative attitudes toward their dad or each other. At the very least, there would be very little love shown to one another in such a family situation.

Jake worked hard every day in the forest. Working for a lumber company cutting, hauling, and cleaning up trees was not a job for the weak or anyone who did not love the outdoors. One thing Jake loved about his job was that he got to see and know the areas where his crew was cutting very well. So he knew where there may be good fishing holes and hunting grounds. When he was given a day off, Jake often explored those possibilities. Hunting and fishing were passions passed on to him from his father and his grandfather.

Jake's wife, Sarah, rarely saw him anymore. During the week, he would leave long before daybreak and come home well into the evening. On weekends, he would be off somewhere with one or more of his buddies traipsing through the same woods that he worked in all week long. Jake lived for the outdoors.

Even when he was asked what he wanted by way of gifts for his birthday or Christmas, it was something from an outdoor supply store: a new fishing rod, a cammy outfit, or some other piece of equipment. Jake was in love with fresh air and new places to check out.

Like so many other women who marry the adventuresome type, Sarah found that her life was a lonely one. If she did not work herself, she would probably go crazy with a lack of attention. At her own place of employment, she could at least have some people to talk to, to share life experience with, or to just enjoy a friendship with. She got very little of those things from Jake.

Because they had no children, the situation did not break up their marriage, but it was not a wonderful one they both wished they could have. It wasn't totally without love but lacked an intimacy they craved.

Jake could continue to go off every weekend and leave Sarah to her loneliness. Sarah could carry on and make the best of the situation but no illusion that it would get much better.

"Living for me" put them on a track of a loveless marriage. It cost them the intimacy, the respect, and the companionship that should be present in any marriage. Too many people are blind to the damage that putting self first does to a relationship.

Mark loved his work at the clinic where he had taken a job as a family physician. His heart was in the work he does. He becomes a friend to each of his clients and gets to know their families. He considers all of them as neighbors. He makes it known to them that he is there to meet their needs, day or night. He is also on call at the hospital for emergencies or to fill in for another doctor who must be away. It is a full but fulfilling schedule. He loves the hours, the people he works with, and his patients. For him, life is good.

In his nonworking hours, Mark spends time building drones and robots. He leads a robotics team of middle school students and loves to be involved in the creative process of designing and building the variety of machines.

Hannah is concerned. Unintentionally, Mark has been spending more and more hours being an engineer and fewer hours being a husband to her and father to their children. She also knows that his time volunteering for the team is eating into what time they might have for intimacy or as a family. This concerns her because she has seen far too many families broken up in similar situations.

Hannah knows that nagging is not the answer. To beg, cry, or manipulate Mark into trying to make her happy would be the wrong thing to do. It would only add to the tension and potentially backfire and cause more harm than good.

One evening when they were both home and the children were occupied with their own activities, she asked Mark if he realized how much time he was spending away from home. Hannah didn't try to put the blame on him to make him feel guilty. She simply asked him to think about the needs of their family. She even suggested that perhaps she could cut back her own hours at the clinic if that would help. When she was done laying out the situation in a calm and reassuring way, Mark could see how much he was needed and how little time he was spending with the very ones God had given him to love, cherish, and protect. He asked her forgiveness and said that he would find a way to cut back on his unnecessary volunteer work. After listening to

Hannah, he realized how much his love for robotics had interfered with their relationship. Together they worked out a future plan of devotion to each other and the children. Both of them realized that volunteering for the sake of keeping busy was not the answer, even if it is something they love to do.

Hobbies or personal pursuits should be fulfilling and rewarding, but when they interfere with relationships, they should be reconsidered. For Mark, it was not necessary to spend so many extra hours with the robotics team. For him, the most important thing is whether or not he is providing the best for his family and at the same time providing needed leadership to the group of kids. He needed to learn to strike a balance.

"Living for me" can cause people to have a warped or unhealthy view of their hobbies or favorite things to do. It can also allow us to spend more time doing the things we love rather than spending quality time with those we have close relationships with. Unconsciously those people become victims rather than partners in our pursuit of pleasure.

Pause and Reflect

What is your favorite thing to do outside of work?

Does it involve other members of the family, or is it a solo project?

Have you ever tracked the amount of time you spend on this hobby or pastime?

If this hobby is a solo venture, how does your significant other feel about the time you spend pursuing this hobby?

Have you ever had to decide between pursuing your hobby and doing something with family? Which way did it go?

Have you ever had to decide between spending money on your favorite pursuit and paying a bill?

Do you know someone whose hobby has become an infatuation or addiction?

Doing an honest reflection on your own fun things to do, are you in danger of becoming addicted?

Have you ever had to talk your spouse/fiancé into doing something with you? Did that person express thoughts of resentment for doing it, or did they thank you?

For the sake of your marriage, would it be better to do things you and your spouse enjoy doing together rather than something you enjoy but your spouse does not?

Adultery

Who doesn't enjoy the exhilaration of a sexual encounter? We are created to enjoy one another's bodies in the union of marriage. However, marriage bonds are no longer seen as sacred and permanent. In our sex-crazed world, there are many opportunities to become unfaithful. People of both genders no longer feel duty bound to put their desires in check to protect or defend their spouse or their marriage union. Most men and women do not think anything of flirtation at the office or on the job. It is a rare place of work where there is not some physical attraction going on, even if it is very brief. Those people who live for themselves find it amusing, laughable, and for some, even acceptable to encourage such activities.

Pat worked in construction. The company he worked for built homes and businesses for clients all over the area. Sometimes they worked in or near his own neighborhood where he lived with his wife, Terry, and their three children. Other times he would be on a jobsite many miles away and stay in a motel until the job was completed rather than commute a long distance.

His responsibility as the supervisor of a crew meant that he had regular contact with the office manager who was an attractive woman who had recently gone through a divorce. It was not unusual for them to flirt with each other either on the phone or while Pat was in the office on business. No one thought much about it.

One day after a major fight with Terry over some matter at home, Pat went to the office in an ugly mood. Sherry, the office manager, was ready and eager to try to console him and offer him encouragement. One thing led to another, and before long, they were seeing each other after work, or she would drive to his motel near a jobsite. What had started as innocent flirtation had developed into an adulterous affair that lasted almost two years until Terry realized what was going on and asked Pat for a divorce.

Sexual attraction is natural. God created us in such a way that we would desire to be together, and part of the attraction is physical. Millions of dollars are spent by people trying to improve their looks in attempts to maintain that attractiveness. There is nothing wrong with that if it is not abused by using bodily attraction to commit sexual sin. God's word is clear that all sexual activity should be restricted to the marriage union.

Louise and Ben have been married for only a year. Before they were wed, Louise knew that Ben had attracted the eye of several other women. In her naiveté, she believed that once they were married, his roving eye would be focused entirely on her. However, she found herself fending off would be lovers by emphatically reminding those ladies that Ben was hers now and he was off-limits. Now after a year of constant battle for his attention, she was almost ready to give up.

Ben was living in a fantasy world of constant attention by the females. Louise was living in a nightmare. As far as anyone knew, there was no physical adultery going on, but the mental strain was as hard to deal with as any affair would have been. The situation left Louise on edge constantly and prevented her from enjoying the intimacy with Ben she desired. Whenever he made love to her, she wondered if she was one of a string or if he truly was committed to her.

No wonder Jesus said that lusting after a woman was as bad as actually taking up with her. Heartache was all that was left as a result of emotional and mental anguish caused by the uncertainty of a spouse's loyalty.

In his practice as a physician, Mark met many attractive women. Two even worked in the office. One in particular had her eye on him. It was no secret that Roberta was attracted to the doctor she spent a lot of time with every day at the clinic.

Roberta would often make what seemed to be innocent remarks that showed her intent. Flirtatious remarks said with a laugh were passed off as a joke. Invitations to parties or events were offered to him with the addendum that he could bring his whole family. Offers to work late with him were made as well as volunteering to go with him on a house call, which he rarely made.

Usually Mark passed them off lightheartedly, taking them at face value. However, one evening after a busy day at the clinic and spending a few hours at the hospital with a patient in critical condition, Mark's defense was down. When Roberta offered to take him home, he took her up on it since Hannah had dropped him off on her way out of town to attend a conference.

The kids were away at camp. The house would be empty, and he needed sleep badly. When they arrived at his home, Roberta saw that he got inside and, taking off her jacket, asked if he would like her to make him a cup of coffee before she left. As tired as he was, Mark clearly got it at that moment. What Roberta wanted was more than he was willing to give. His love and loyalty to Hannah were strong enough for him to ask Roberta to leave.

He promised her that if she left and did not pursue this line of thinking and action, nothing more would be said and it would be behind them. No one else needed to know what her intentions had been. He would guard her dignity if she would respect his marriage. Reluctantly, Roberta saw the high level of this man's integrity and love. She realized then that true love looks out for its own and to break that commitment would be very difficult.

After that, Roberta's respect for Mark was even greater than before. She even developed the attitude that it was a real pleasure to work with a man of such a high level of integrity, which for her was very rare.

Mark's actions, even though he found Roberta attractive, were taken with his family in mind. If he had desired to fulfill his base-level desires, they would have spent the night together, perhaps leading to more in the future, which in turn could have had dire consequences once the facts were made known. But out of love for Hannah and his children, Mark refused to yield to the temptation to please himself. That refusal showed how strong the bond was between him and Hannah and between him and God. Both of these relationships were worth much more than a night of self-fulfillment of temporary desires.

The next time he and Hannah had a talk, Mark even told her what had happened. He apologized for seemingly posing a threat to their marriage by possibly acting inappropriately at the office. Hannah said that she understood how Roberta could be attracted to him given his good looks and his (supposedly) good income. She then thanked him for standing up for her and their vows. To be loved so strongly by a man who faces such tempting opportunities every day is an honor.

Adultery is a trap that is so easy to fall into. The opportunities are prevalent and frequent. Pastors and other church leaders are not immune. Youth workers are placed in high-risk positions for flirtations and sexual sin. It is when selfish desire takes control that these people fall and that consequences are severe. No one is shielded from the advances of those who are trying to meet their own pleasures, but all of us are called to self-control and to stand firm in our allegiances, either to our spouses or to our God who holds us to a higher standard than the rest of the world does.

"Living for me" says we can find pleasure wherever we can find it. Living for the Lord and with our commitments in mind means we put our own pleasure on the back burner in favor of pleasing others. When there comes a time of sexual temptation, we should remember that we have a responsibility to "keep the marriage bed pure" (Hebrews 13:4).

Pause and Reflect

Who do you know who has been involved with adultery?

What happened?

How did the innocent party handle the situation?

From a biblical perspective, do you think it is better for the innocent party to fight for the marriage or immediately ask for a divorce?

What steps can a couple take to remedy the situation?

Many couples try counseling from a pastor or professional. At what point do you think this should begin: when the affair is first uncovered or after they try to resolve it themselves?

Is it selfish for a woman (which is usually the case) to demand the loyalty of her husband, even if the marriage is not a happy one?

When a spouse strays, does he or she fall victim to another person's charms, or is he or she fulfilling selfish desires consciously or unconsciously?

How seriously should a couple take their vows made before God and those in attendance at their wedding? How would this help prevent adultery?

Pornography

Pornography is rampant. Sexually explicit photos are everywhere. It is a blind person who does not see them portrayed on television and the internet, as well as in the traditional places like magazines and flyers. It has always been a mantra of advertising that sex sells. Every major media outlet uses sex to sell everything from toothpaste to vacations and clothes. This has always been the case. What is more evident in our interconnected world are the graphic depictions in the airwaves that are not easily controlled by any government agency which doesn't matter much anyway, since the rules that govern such filth have been relaxed over the years.

With the intervention of the internet into our homes and offices, and now even our pockets, the opportunities to view pornography have skyrocketed. Those persons who have access to such filth without anyone else present are the most susceptible since there is no one to hold them accountable. They must learn to police themselves and their viewing habits. That is not easy when invitations pop up regularly right in front of our faces.

Gunther had no intention of being a pornography addict. He loved his wife, Leah, and his four children. Working at a small local glass business, he was often left alone while the others went out on jobs. It was his responsibility to answer calls, take orders, and be sure the proper materials were on hand when a job was scheduled. He was not the office manager, officially, but did a lot of the office work so the rest of the guys could focus on meeting the customers' needs. There were many days when there was not much on schedule for him, so it left him with a lot of idle time.

The company had a "no personal use" rule relating to the computer, but everyone broke the rule regularly. Some of the guys would look up places to go on vacation so their wives wouldn't know beforehand. Others often researched things relating to purchases they wanted to make and so on. No one enforced the rule at all, although everyone understood that if they were caught, it could mean the loss of their job.

Gunther would sometimes search for a good place to buy a gift for his wife or one of the kids for their birthday. Instead of waiting to get home to use his personal computer, he would go online during a down time at work. When he did, the inevitably enticing pictures would begin to infiltrate his viewing space. He always ignored them, completed his business, and logged off before he was caught. But one day, it didn't happen that way.

As Gunther was prowling around on the internet, he accidentally clicked on one of those alluring photos, which took him to a web page full of sexually explicit pictures. He didn't stay long, but the effect was long-lasting. The images kept playing over and over in his head. Another day, he found himself going back without waiting for the invitation. He stayed a little longer. Before long, he was visiting pornographic web sites as often as he could, both at work and at home. It got to the point where he would even stay up at night after his family had gone to bed, pretending to be on a social media page. He would spend a couple of hours viewing women attempting to make him enjoy his visit.

Gunther didn't realize how bad the situation was until his wife caught him one night and confronted him about his addiction. Gunther defended himself by saying it was a manly thing to look at women. There was nothing wrong that he could see. Didn't all *real* men do that?

Leah tried to plead with him to back off from viewing those sites, claiming it was not good and that it set a poor example for their children. She attempted to get him into counseling, but Gunther denied he had a problem. This went on for more than a year until the office computer needed servicing. When the company technician cleaned the computer and found that Gunther had been accessing such sites, it was his duty to inform the company directors. That resulted in Gunther being fired.

But that did not prevent his habit at home from continuing. Eventually Leah had had enough and asked Gunther to either get some help or get out. Because he still did not grasp the strength of his addiction, he said he would try to get help. But that did not last and finally he chose to leave so he could pursue his addiction without her nagging him.

"Living to please me" has consequences, and they are not usually good. Gunther has lost his job, his marriage, and his dignity, among other things. But his desire to please himself is so strong he couldn't stop it. He has fallen into the trap of putting himself and his satisfaction ahead of everything else.

Gunther is not alone. There are literally millions of men and women who have followed this path of self-destruction. It is one of Satan's most effective tools, and he uses it as often as he can, which is why we see scantily clad models and celebrities so frequently. Sexual addictions start with seemingly innocent flirtations or exposure. We are then drawn in to see more and experience more, either vicariously through the media or actually by means of those who provide willing partners.

Sam was not socially active. When he was not at work, he rarely interacted with other people outside of his home. One of his favorite pastimes was to read. Having learned to read at a young age, Sam loved to dive into a novel, a short story, or anything that happened to be lying around. He was one the few people who actually read old magazines at the doctor's office.

Whenever he and Dawn visited a flea market or yard sale, he would always come home with a book or two. Once he found a whole box for very little money. He couldn't pass up such a bargain.

The problem with his reading habit was the he was not very discriminatory about what he read. He did learn to distinguish those authors he enjoyed and marked as his favorites. But often he would buy some written by unknown authors. One such book seemed appealing by its cover and promised story line, but as he got into it, the action went from casual and fun reading to flagrant sexual action. Sam felt somewhat disgusted by the descriptive language and the way the story was developing but didn't seem to have the fortitude to put it down. He read the book through to the end but felt dirty in his mind for a long time. The images plagued him for months afterward.

The sad thing was that there was a certain level of excitement from reading that kind of book. Soon Sam found himself seeking out more of that kind of material. When Dawn discovered what kind of books he was reading, she had a fit. Not only did she warn Sam that it was not good entertainment, but she did not want that kind of material lying around where the children could read it for themselves. As is the case with most addicts, Sam denied the negative impact it was making on his own mind or his relationship with Dawn.

Trying to please his own desires and feed his addiction, Sam let his reading habit build a wall between him and his family. "Living for me" could cost him dearly if he did not find help to deal with this monster in their home. He now had a choice: either give up his unhealthy habit or give up the woman and family that God had given him to love, honor, and cherish.

In Mark's busy schedule, there is no time to spend idly on the computer or to look at sexually explicit magazines or literature. His day is filled with appointments, hospital rounds, and staff meetings. By the time he arrives home, all he wants is to unwind with a cool drink. Sometimes he will watch a TV show while he is waiting for Hannah to arrive. Other times he will pick up the kids and take them to games or concerts after school. So Mark rarely has opportunities to be sucked into the world of pornography. But rarely does not mean never.

One day he didn't feel well so he stayed home from the clinic to rest and take some flu medicine, thinking it would go away with treatment. Late that morning, the house was quiet and he couldn't sleep anymore so he decided to flip through the channels on the TV to find something to watch. As he did so, he came across an alluring ad for a sexually explicit program. He immediately switched to another on the list. However, that image stuck in his mind, and having noted the time for the show was only a few minutes away, his curiosity was piqued. His conscience said to forget it and shut off the television or watch a more family-oriented channel. His curiosity told him it wouldn't hurt just to check it out just once and if he didn't like it to never do it again. He mentally wrestled with the decision for a brief while, but finally curiosity won over conscience.

Wrapped in a blanket on the couch with the house all to himself, Mark felt at that moment that no one would ever have to know what he was watching and that it would be a one-time event. Little did he realize the power of pornography. The sexual stimulation and elation of watching others expose themselves and offer their bodies for pleasure made him feel really good. When the show was over, he turned off the television and tried to take a nap, feeling the effects of the drugs he had taken earlier. As he lay back with his eyes closed, all he could see in his mind were the scenes of the show he had just watched. His mind wanted to play them over and over.

He lay there with a tortured mind. Selfishly he wanted to go back and watch some more. He tried to rationalize not telling Hannah, thinking there was no real harm done to her or the family. However, he knew that God was not pleased with what he had done, even this once. He knew also that it could change the way he viewed his relationship with Hannah, reducing her to an object of his pleasures. Realizing the seriousness of the situation, he purposely prayed to God for forgiveness. He also asked God to give him wisdom to ask Hannah's forgiveness and support to find ways to prevent future incidences.

Finally, believing he was on the path of putting this behind him, Mark fell asleep. He slept restfully for about an hour and woke up with a sense of peace. Immediately upon awakening, he contacted the television provider service and asked how to put a block on their set to prevent any future access to such shows. The support person was very helpful and walked him through the steps. Having done that, Mark then spent the next hour reading his Bible, seeking verses that would help him to resist temptations. He took notes of those he thought might be helpful.

At noontime, Hannah came home to share her lunch hour with him and to check on him. When they had finished eating, he confessed to her what had happened. He related how he ended up watching such a show and asked her to forgive him because it showed a lack of respect for her and other women. They talked about it for a few minutes, and when he told her that he had already taken steps to prevent it happening again, she thanked him and said how much she admired his bravery in doing that. She knew how easily someone can get caught up in such degrading expositions. Several families she dealt with had been broken up partly for that very reason. They both had seen it happen in their church when a youth pastor had fallen victim to this same alluring trap. It had cost him personally and the church dearly as well.

Mark took the steps against future involvement for two good reasons. First, he loved Hannah and would never hurt her intentionally. She was his whole world, next to God, and he wanted to do whatever it took to keep her love and respect. Second, Mark knew that God was not pleased with what he had done and to do what he could to prevent any future temptations would also be pleasing to the Lord. Such actions showed that he wanted to live more for Hannah and the Lord than for himself.

The practical step Mark and Hannah took together to make this a one-time event were good, but they did not take away the impact on Mark's mind. People think you can watch something and soon forget it. That may be true of some things, but when Satan wants to entrap you, to tease you, or to make you feel guilty, he will not let those nasty scenes fade from your mind any time soon. They may actually be recalled many years later if the conditions are right. The act of the sin may have been forgiven and the potential disaster averted, but the temptation is still there with you. Every time the enemy brings it to your attention, you need to ask God to give you the strength to resist and to live for His pleasure, not your own. See 1 Corinthians 10:13.

Pause and Reflect

What, in your opinion, makes sex so attractive?

Have you ever been attracted to sexually explicit material?

Do you know anyone who has developed a habit or an addiction to such material?

Has anyone you know sought counseling for being attracted or addicted to pornography? What was the result?

Are there other habits that can become addictive as pornography? What are they?

Why do believe addictions are so hard to break?

Having an accountability partner is necessary to overcome most bad habits. How can a spouse or lover be a good accountability partner?

What might make them a poor one?

As Christians, we all have someone we are accountable to: the Lord Jesus. Why is knowing this not enough for most people to avoid or be set free from addictions?

Any addiction is self-satisfying. If our purpose in life is to please God in everything we do, how can we justify a selfish habit?

Parental
Responsibilities

When we become parents, our world changes forever. It is no longer just the two of us who share the home. As a family, it is no longer you and me but the three or more of us. In fact, finding time for just the two of us may be something we will have to learn to work into our increasingly busy schedules. Most couples welcome the little ones into their lives with joy and excitement. The anticipation of becoming first-time parents builds agonizingly slowly until the child arrives. Sometime later, reality sets in. All our time away from work seems to be centered around and focused on the children. For some parents, this is not a problem because they expected to assume this role even before they knew children were in their future. Others though find that the reality of nurturing, training, and attending to the children takes away from personal goals and desires. Those who see their offspring as a nuisance find ways to set them aside for their own selfish pleasures or careers.

Ethan and Jane were such a couple. When their first child, a girl, was born, they had already planned out what they were going to do. Since Ethan was a member of a busy law firm, he was needed at the office every day and sometimes well into the evening to handle cases. Jane, for her part, was a schoolteacher who loved her job and wouldn't miss a day if she could help it. She had her sights set on becoming an administrator in the local school system. To reach that goal, not only did she teach every day, but she also took classes at night to attain the necessary degree for the position she desired.

When Jane discovered she was pregnant, there was no real debate on what they were going to do. Even before Janet was born, they had lined up a capable childcare worker to take care of her during the day or whenever neither of them could be there. Ethan and Jane thought the money they paid for such service was worth the investment to help their respective careers along. As Janet grew, she was constantly in daycare or under the care of a sitter, seeing her own parents only for a few minutes on some evenings but not at all on most.

Even after she was in school and participated in after-school activities, it was the sitter or an aunt or uncle who was there for her. Very seldom did one of her parents come to a game or hear her play in the band. For Ethan and Jane, their own needs came before those of their child. They loved Janet, but more in the way of loving a pet than a family member.

The whole situation came to a head one day when Jane came home to find eleven-year-old Janet alone. There was a note from the sitter to say that she had a family emergency and had to leave. Janet had been instructed to lock the doors and all the windows, to stay inside, and not to answer the phone unless she recognized the voice on the answering machine. All these things Janet did without question. The problem was the liquor cabinet was not locked and Janet decided to see why her parents were so insistent to go there almost every evening when they got home. When she had tasted some wine, she decided she liked the fruity flavor so she drank a whole glass of it. By the time Jane arrived, Janet had fallen asleep on the couch, spilling the remainder of the bottle on the rug.

A couple of years later, by being pretty much her own boss, Janet came home high on drugs and her father discovered that this was not the first time she had been abusing at parties and at school. This made Ethan furious. He accused Janet of ruining his reputation and standing in the community. He could not understand why his daughter would do such things when he provided so much for her. Jane was almost as mad as Ethan. She did not yell but made it very clear that Janet's actions could possibly prevent her mother from getting the advancements in the school system she worked so long and hard for. Both of them were blind to the needs of Janet.

Christopher and Andrea were expecting their third child. Christopher was proud of his children and bragged to everyone what a wonderful wife he had. Together they were making things work. Even though Andrea had to stop working to be there for the children, they managed to get by on the proverbial shoestring. But all was not well in their household.

Andrea was a loving, caring mom who did the best she could for her children. There were two problems that she had to deal with. One was that she had very little education and came from a home where love was rarely shown. Discipline usually consisted of yelling, cursing, or grabbing an arm to get a child's attention. There was very little positive reinforcement to nurture the young minds in a positive direction. The other problem was her desire for creating a line of jewelry. Most of time was spent either crafting the pieces or online promoting them to shoppers. Whenever the children interfered, she would make it plain that she did not appreciate being interrupted. This made for a long, tiring, and stressful day. By the time Christopher got home from work in the evening, Andrea was ready to let him take over.

Christopher did his best to show love and compassion to the children and at the same time not let them get away with unruly behavior, but being with them only for a few hours in the evening did not offset the lack of parental control the entire day. It was a losing battle he fought for the well-being of the children he loved so dearly.

After the oldest child had begun school, it was suspected that child abuse was evident, so the authorities were called. It truly broke Christopher's heart to go through the process of dealing with the child welfare office. In the end, it was decided that the children would benefit from a better environment so they were removed from the home.

Children need parents who care about them, love them without reservation, and do what is necessary to help them become productive, caring adults in their own right. Without adult supervision and guidance, children are left to fend for themselves in a cruel world which does not, for the most part, care how their character turns out. If the majority of the children in a given generation are neglected like Janet was or not given much parental supervision, it is no wonder our drug abuse rates, our crime statistics, and the level of immorality will continue to remain high or even get worse. Praise God there are parents who still care enough for their children's character development to do what it takes to teach them personal responsibility, respect for authority, and right from wrong.

As busy as they were with their respective medical practices, Mark and Hannah determined early that they would not have their children reared by nonfamily members. For the first few years, while the children were small, they were left with a caretaker during the day, but before the day began, it was understood who would pick them up after work and spend time with them before the evening meal. A plan was worked out that Hannah could do it three days of the week and Mark could do it two, giving them both plenty of opportunity to spend quality time with the little ones. After the evening meal, the babies were usually tired enough to put to bed so the two of them would have the evening to themselves except when an emergency call came in. Saturdays were family days unless there was a prior commitment. Sundays were reserved for worship and family outings. On those two days, the whole family was together all day barring any emergency calls or if Mark was in rotation to take a weekend shift at the hospital.

Later, when afternoon naps had been outgrown and school became a part of the routine, instead of shuttling them off to a sitter, they would stay with Hannah's dad or an aunt living nearby. Extracurricular activities were not so easy to work into their hectic schedules, but somehow they made it work. Over and over again they assured each of their children that they would be there for them as much as possible.

One thing they did when a child announced he or she wanted to participate in sports, band, or some other activity was to have a family discussion about it. This made each of the children realize that everything they decided to do also affects everyone else in the family. No one was allowed to do as he pleased without considering how it changed the schedule, impacted the family budget, and created a logistic puzzle that had to be solved. Mark and Hannah never said no to anything worthwhile but showed the children through reason, discussion, and experience that we are not in this world to do just as we please.

By including the children in such discussions and planning sessions, they learned early how to respect other people's opinions, see things from different perspectives, and that nothing comes without a cost. Very seldom did either Mark or Hannah have to assert their authority to negate a decision. Usually the child could see whether or not it had a negative impact on the rest of the family, and when it was understood that to join in on a particular project was unproductive or just not workable, the child would accept the fact that he could not do it.

Mark and Hannah did not try to make every game, match, or competition a child was involved in, and the children knew why. However, whenever they could, they would be there, especially when one of them was on a team that was in a playoff or championship. They knew that parental support was very important. But more than that, the process their family used showed love and respect for the children as individuals, which was reciprocated. No one was left out, and no one had unequal rights. They were all listened to and had a voice in the family decision process. The children learned a sense of personal value early, and it grew as they did. They matured into young adults with a set of morals, a mind-set that put a value on others, and they saw their own ability to contribute positively to the world around them.

For their part, Mark and Hannah were not so self-pleasing that they would refuse to be involved in the lives of their offspring. Rather, they accepted them as a part of their lives with joy. The children did not demand things or their own way (not very often anyway) because they were taught early to share and let others go first. "Living for me" was never even entertained in their household. Whenever that ugly monster reared its ugly head, it was quickly lopped off because no one wanted to hurt others in the process of pleasing themselves. The love bond was too strong for that.

Pause and Reflect

What observations have you made from watching parents interact with children? Have you noticed differing nurturing styles?

If you have children of your own, how would you describe your style?

In your opinion, what amount of time is reasonable for a child to be under the care of someone other than their own parents?

What plans have you made for the care of any children you have or may have?

How would those plans affect your employment? Would you or your spouse stop working or put your children in the care of others while you work?

The Bible tells us that parents have the responsibility of training children "in the way they should go." How can we do that if we are not there for them in their formative years?

Vacations

When did the definition of a vacation change? When did it switch from a time to relax and not worry about everyday responsibilities to being full of anxiety and activity to get to some place or do something that usually doesn't go as planned?

Whenever my wife and I announce we are taking a vacation, everyone immediately asks, "Where are you going? What are your plans?" We have to simply say, "We have none. We plan to just kick back and take one day at a time, enjoying each other's company for a few days." I know that is probably rare, but it's what we do. Others fall into the trap of spending untold hours planning a time away and find that the planning process is as hectic as work itself. Then they get to wherever and find there is too much going on to really relax.

Justin and Angela had decided to take a vacation from work to get away. Both of them looked forward to a time of relaxation, fun, and reduced responsibilities. They would pack up the SUV and the kids and be off for a week of adventure. But that was as far as their agreement went.

Justin had his heart set on spending time at a remote lake camping, fishing, canoeing, and enjoying the fresh air. He knew just the spot because his dad had taken him and his family there many times while he was young. Now he wanted to take his own family there to relive those experiences. Without consulting Angela, he went ahead and booked the campsite well in advance.

After work one day, he went to the local outfitter's store and purchased the gear they would need to go camping. When he arrived home, he put it all in the garage, waiting to load it into the SUV just before they left. When Angela found out, she was very upset. She did not want to go camping. Being an active woman, she did not relish the idea of spending time away from civilization and sleeping in a tent, and she certainly was *not* looking forward to cooking every meal for a week over a camp stove or a fire pit. She had her own plans.

She thought it would be better to go to a family resort so the kids could be entertained by their favorite movie characters or television stars. They could spend every day actively engaged in rides, shows, or swimming in the hotel pool. Moreover, she would not have to cook a single meal. She had ordered brochures and information to share with the children to prepare them for what was to be a fun-filled week. The tickets and the hotel were already reserved.

Planning a family vacation takes time and open discussion. Justin and Angela both wanted the family to enjoy what they selfishly wanted: him to go back to his roots and her to be as free from domestic responsibilities as much as possible. They were both thinking about themselves. Neither of them considered what the other may have had in mind. The only thing they had talked about and acted on together was the timing of the vacation. Other than that, each of them assumed they had the right or responsibility to plan it. Now they were booked to go in two different directions. What were they to do?

Obviously one of them had to concede to the other or they could cancel both plans and start over. The problem was the day to leave was almost upon them and they had very little time to change plans. Justin understood where Angela was coming from when she planned the resort vacation, and Angela accepted the fact that Justin wanted to allow the children an opportunity to connect with their dad's heritage. But that didn't help resolve the situation.

Justin argued that to go back to nature would cost a lot less than spending a week at a resort, considering they would have to pay for every meal on top of the exorbitant price for the room. It would set them back a great deal financially. He also resented the fact that Angela had already told the children where they would be going and getting them all excited about it. He didn't think it was fair to him for her to do that.

Angela's argument was that even though it may cost more, they would have comfortable rooms to sleep in, good food to eat, and plenty to do with little chance of getting bored. She would be free to give her full attention to him and the children. They could even stay caught up with the laundry and not drag home a pile of dirty clothes. She didn't think Justin should ask her and the children to do something they may not enjoy. What about the bugs, hard ground under the sleeping bags, or the remoteness of the campsite? What would they do on a rainy day? There were 101 reasons she could think of to not go camping.

They argued about it for several days. Finally Justin gave in, but not without a promise from Angela that they would agree to go camping on their next summer vacation when the children were a little older. He carried his resentment with him for a long time afterward. Every time he went into the garage and saw the camping gear, he was reminded how Angela had undermined his plans. It remained a sore spot that didn't heal.

For Angela, it was a hollow victory. She had gotten her way, but she had pushed Justin away a little bit. She could feel the disappointment in his attitude as they continued to prepare to go. When a decision had to be made, he told her since she had set this up, she could handle it all. He would come along, but not willingly. He would be there for the sake of the kids, not to feed Angela's selfish pleasures.

The tension between them had prevented them from experiencing the freedom, fun, and relaxation they had anticipated. The children had been demanding and sometimes unruly, asking for things. Daily decisions were often the trigger for an argument. Justin cringed every time he had to reach for his wallet to pay for something not originally in their plans. When they finally arrived back home, neither of them could honestly say they had enjoyed themselves.

Rick and his wife, Debbie, planned well in advance for their annual time away. They did this every year because they knew from experience that careful planning was the key to a great vacation. This year they were going on a road trip across America, something they had both wanted to do for a long time. Now they had saved enough to afford it and were excited about the trip.

What they had hoped to be an enjoyable adventure on some of America's back roads turned out to be more drudgery than fun. Every morning it was decision time. Which road do we take? Where do we stop for meals? What sights do we want to take in today? They almost never could agree on the answers. Rick would want to go in one direction and Debbie in another. He wanted to have local food for lunch or dinner when she would always insist they find a fast-food place to save money. Every afternoon they would have to try to locate a good place to park the motor home for the night. That too sparked a daily debate. All of their detailed planning amounted to nothing when something didn't go according to the plan. Things like a three-day rainstorm, a blown tire in the middle of nowhere, or a minor illness that required a doctor disrupted their itinerary and forced them to make changes. When they arrived back home two weeks later, they were both exhausted and glad to be back. The pressure of each one trying to get his or her own way made the trip more of a nightmare than the dream they had when they left.

Mark and Hannah had also planned a family vacation. They sat down together one evening and selected a week that would work for them both. They also discussed many different options open to them. After thinking and brainstorming together, they narrowed down the choices to three. They could take the children for an outdoor trip to the mountains and occupy a cabin by a lake, they could go to a beach resort and spend the time doing ocean activities, or they could just spend the week at home going on day trips to different venues in their own area seeing sights, visiting museums, or attending various shows and events within a half-day drive.

The next day, they presented the plans to the children and asked them what they thought about each of the options. They discussed what each one would involve, including sleeping arrangements, what activities were available, and what expenses were attached. Mark and Hannah wanted this to be a true family vacation, not one to please either of the adults or one child over the wishes of the other.

When they realized that a consensus could not be reached immediately, they asked the children to think about the options and come back later with their decisions. They had plenty of time to make plans.

Because the children had been included in family decisions before, they knew that even if their personal choice was not the final option chosen, they would accept it. All of them understood and learned early that it was not about getting your own way but making plans that would benefit the whole family. One by one, each came back with the decision they had made. Hannah and Mark took their thoughts into consideration. In the end, they decided as a family where to go and what to do.

Because each respected other family members' opinions no matter where they went, they knew they would enjoy it without bickering, arguing, or holding any regrets or grudges. When they returned from a week away in the mountains, they brought with them fond memories, exciting stories to share with friends and family, and lots and lots of pictures with smiling faces. No one came home regretting the decision they had made.

Living to please me can destroy family unity and drain relationships of respect, nurture, and love. On the other hand, living to please others or for the common good can foster an attitude of joy, pleasure, and fun.

Pause and Reflect

Do you have memories of vacationing with your parents? Are they fond memories or scary ones?

What kind of memories would you like your children to have of time spent together as a family?

As adults, we often plan things without including the children and usually end up doing adult stuff with the children tagging along. Is that fair?

What is the process like in your home to plan a family vacation?

What kinds of things have to be considered in the planning to make it work? Length? Finances? Experiences? Location?

How can your knowledge of God or the Bible guide you in making decisions relating to a family outing?

Does God even care where you go or what you do as a family?

Volunteering

Volunteering for good cause isn't about me, is it? It sets a good example for my family, right? Dick would say it can be selfishly motivated, and it does not always set a great example.

Dick and Wendy had been searching for a church to join. When they found an active congregation only a couple of miles from their home, they felt welcomed right away. Soon it was apparent to Wendy that she could be of help with the young children since she only worked part time at her job and had plenty of time to commit to them.

At first it was only as a backup Sunday school teacher, meaning she only had to be there when the regular teacher had to be away or was sick. Before long, she was in the classroom every week as a helper as well. This was fine with Dick. He didn't mind Wendy's involvement at all. In fact, he thought it was a good idea because this would help her keep busy in her spare time.

Wendy was the kind of person who took every one's problems to heart. When one of the children expressed a need, she was the first one to jump in and try to help. That meant she did a lot of one-on-one talking and listening. It also meant that she would buy clothes or a box of food or pay for something she believed the child or his family desperately needed.

Dick took all this in stride since he could see that it meant a lot to Wendy to be needed and to be someone who was there for these kids, many of whom had no one to love them or show any kind of attention.

After doing this for about a year, an opportunity came for Wendy to join a civic group dedicated to the needs of children in the community. She jumped at the chance. As she saw it, this would give her more resources to help even more kids and their families. She wanted to be of help in any way that she could. This position brought her to the attention of other organization leaders, and before she knew it, Wendy had been placed on the board of five such groups in her area, and one of them was a state level position. What had started out as a simple part-time volunteer position had developed into a full schedule of meetings, travel, and overseeing other volunteers. At the end of each week, Wendy was exhilarated but exhausted.

In the meantime, Dick was seeing less and less of his wife. What started out as an occasional absence for the evening meal became a regular thing. More times than not when he came home from work, Dick would have to deal with the children's needs, provide a meal for them, and try to relax before retiring for the night. Wendy would often come home well into the night, sometimes after he had gone to bed. It was not very often the two of them had any time alone anymore.

One day when it so happened that he had a day off and she did not have to be anywhere until evening, he confronted Wendy about the situation. He expressed to her that he understood her desire to be of help to as many people as possible but that he felt that she was neglecting her family. He suggested that perhaps she could cut back on her volunteering a little for the sake of their marriage and the children's needs. This did not go over well.

Wendy's immediate reaction was that she was not only doing it for the victims of poverty, neglect, or abuse, but it also helped her develop skills and abilities. She felt somewhat fulfilled through these activities. Would Dick really want her to sit at home and not use her gifts to help others? Would he insist on holding her back from doing good when Jesus had said that doing good was a benefit to his kingdom? She played the guilt card very deftly and carefully. Dick fell for it and let the matter drop.

Later, however, as he was walking down the hall of their

home, he wondered as he passed a panel of awards, citations, and certificates if what Wendy was doing was so much for the sake of the children anymore but really for herself. Perhaps the temporary volunteer position had morphed into a monster of self-promotion. Wendy, as far as he could tell, rarely spent any time with individual clients but worked among those who made the decisions that governed the ministries or agencies that provided the resources and personnel. She no longer had the time to be a help in the Sunday school class. This monster was killing their marriage.

He knew it was useless to try to talk to Wendy about it. She was as stubborn as she was compassionate. The only thing he knew to do to get her attention was to take drastic steps. So one day when Wendy came home after yet another long day of meetings and conferences that lasted well into the evening, the house was dark with a note on the front door saying that Dick and the kids were gone. If she wanted to see them again, she would have to come to where they were and apologize for her frequent absences and pledge to cut back. Otherwise, it was over.

Wendy was truly living for herself. She was being fulfilled as a woman, as a volunteer, and as a leader. Being a part of these many groups made her feel good; it made her feel wanted and even needed. She didn't know when the shift had come, but somewhere along the way, her focus had changed from wanting to help people with names and faces to wanting to do all she can and receive applause and recognition. Every time she walked down that hall in their home, she felt a sense of pride and accomplishment. The world was better off because of her activities and these trophies proved it. The monster of self-gratification had won.

But all the trophies in the world are not worth the cost of a marriage or of relationships that are valuable to us. "Living for me" has consequences. Wendy now had to face those consequences and decide which was more important to her: her family or her self-fulfillment through volunteering.

Dale too fell into the trap of the allure of helping. Since he retired, he has spent almost all of his waking moments volunteering for one cause or another. He held memberships in four fraternal clubs that did charitable work on a regular basis. When he was not involved in one of those he volunteered at the local residential home for seniors. His wife, Lois, rarely saw him at all except on those evenings when he did not have a club meeting.

One day Lois was hospitalized for an infection. Dale saw that she was settled in and was well tended to. However, all the while he was with her, he was receiving calls or text messages about the planned activities on his calendar. Most of his time was spent returning calls or messages to let his team members know what to do or who to contact relating to the upcoming event. Lois felt like she was confined to a busy office rather than a hospital. Dale was blind to the emotional needs of his wife while concentrating on the larger needs of the community or the organizations for which he volunteered.

When he was asked why he spent so much time doing good for others, he always replied that it kept him active and made him feel good. He never complained about the work or the hours of commitment. Although he would deny it, Dale was living for himself. He was doing the charity work because of what he could get out of it. He loved the idea that this name was known all over town for his work. It made him feel good all right, but it made Lois feel extremely lonely.

Hannah too spent time volunteering at various events, especially at the schools where her children were enrolled. There were plenty of times when there was a fundraiser, a play, a concert, or some other project that demanded an army of volunteers to make it happen. Most of the time, parents, primarily moms, were recruited to fill those roles. Hannah was no exception.

However, in Hannah's case, she did not take on any project or activity that would interfere with her work as a nurse, her family time at home, or her relationship with her husband. Like everything else, when an opportunity came up that she might be interested in, she would mention it in their family discussions and get feedback from the other members of the family. Sometimes it worked out, and sometimes it did not. Hannah chose not to jeopardize her family relationships to chase some temporary pride for a job well done. The projects all seemed to get along just fine, whether or not she was involved. The ugly monster "living for me" that had consumed the life of Wendy did not even live at Hannah's house. He had never been welcomed there and when discovered was soon sent packing.

Pause and Reflect

Have you volunteered at church or some other organization? If so, did you enjoy the experience?

Do you know someone who volunteers on a regular basis? Does that person appear to enjoy what they do or accept it as a job that needs to be done?

Does anyone you know volunteer for more than one project long term? How does that seem to affect that person's relationship with family members?

Can volunteering become an addiction? What would trigger such an outcome?

The Bible heavily emphasizes the concept of helping others. Is there such a thing as doing too much?

Have you ever known a couple whose relationship was broken due to one person spending so much time helping others or volunteering for causes?

How can a person balance what God expects by way of helping others and the need to maintain a healthy relationship with our spouses and family?

Elderly or Needy
Family Members

We all hear about elder abuse. Usually that conjures up visions of beatings or neglect in residential facilities. But what about the older members of families who are not given the kind of care they so desperately need?

Mr. and Mrs. Hannibal were elderly and in frail health. Like so many in their age group, time had not been kind to them physically, and now they needed physical and medical attention a lot. Up until now, they had been able to maintain their own home, but with Mrs. Hannibal's declining health due to dementia, they were finding it more and more difficult to keep up the work of maintaining the home and to pay the bills. There were times when she did not remember to pay a utility bill or found it difficult to keep the checkbook balanced. Her husband tried his best to help her and did a lot of the housework. But they both knew that this could not continue.

Their son, Maurice, lived near them with his wife and three children ranging in ages from four to eight. They were a busy family as most are with children in that age group. There were commitments to work, school, and church activities. Quality family time was reserved for an occasional outing. Now with his parents in need of extra help, the burden would become even heavier.

One day when he was visiting with them, Maurice could see

for himself how far the situation had deteriorated. His mother had difficulty preparing lunch for her and his dad, who was temporarily confined to an easy chair with breathing issues. This woke him up to the need for someone to assist them. He knew who their primary doctor was, so he called and asked for a referral to an agency that might be able to help.

Maurice's wife, Beth, would squeeze in a visit from time to time to check on them and to do some of the housework. She also made sure they were taking their medicines as prescribed.

While they waited for a return call from the nursing agency, Maurice talked with Beth about the situation. He made it clear that he would not bring them into their home, even for a short while. He reasoned that with their busy lifestyle, the responsibility for his parents' welfare would be more than they could handle.

There would be more frequent visits to the doctor, extra laundry, higher grocery bills, and no chance for them to spend time away without wondering what to do with the old folks. He was in favor of having the nursing agency or their family doctor seek out a senior housing facility or a rehabilitation center where they could be in a safe setting and under the watchful care of trained personnel. He did not want the burden of their care on his shoulders. He would rather be free to visit them or not in another place, not in his own home.

Beth agreed. To have them come live with them would be a terrible situation. She would end up being their primary caregiver, which would mean that in addition to tending to the needs of her family, these two elderly people would occupy a lot of her time. She would rarely have time to do the things she liked to do, such as volunteering and going out with her lady friends once in a while. She would not be free to pursue her own pleasures or goals as long as they were in the home.

So it was settled. It was only a matter of a short while before a place was found that met the needs of Maurice's parents. He and his family helped them move into their new apartment. When the unpacking was all done, Maurice and Beth, with the children, sighed with relief, thinking they had done a good deed for his parents. At the same time, there was very little disruption of their life as a family.

For the Hannibals, the decision was based entirely on what was best for them, not Maurice's parents. Whether they ended up in an assisted living center, a nursing home, or hospital didn't really matter to Maurice. All he and Beth really wanted was to be free from this burden that his parents created by being old and infirm. They passed the responsibility off onto someone else so they could be free to pursue their own pleasures.

Maurice and Beth separated themselves from the older generation, and their children, after this transition, never had a chance to interact with their grandparents the way they could have. Visits became fewer and fewer. Almost never did the children accompany one of the parents when they stopped in to see them in their new environment. When they finally passed away, the grandchildren hardly knew who their grandparents were.

Mark and Hannah faced a similar situation with Hannah's dad. Her mother had passed away shortly after Hannah had graduated college, but her dad was still living in the old house the last few years. In the meantime, Mark and Hannah had moved to another home a few miles away. Now his health was failing. He hardly left the house anymore except to run errands or go see his doctor. Even then, he would find someone, usually a neighbor, to drive him where he needed to go.

One day in a phone conversation with Hannah, he mentioned that he was thinking of finding some other place to live that would be less costly and less difficult to maintain. He told her that his rheumatoid arthritis was getting so bad he could hardly move some days. He realized he could not care for himself without help much longer. He wasn't asking for help from her but stating what he saw as reality.

Hannah, as soon as an opportunity arose, shared the situation with Mark. She knew what their own busy lives entailed and that having her father living with them would create an extra burden, but she wanted to find out how Mark felt about it. As the two of them discussed the options open to her dad, they agreed that they did not want to put him away in isolation in an elderly living unit of any kind. He was family and family looked out for one another.

There was no discussion about what kind of sacrifice they may have to make if they brought him into their home. The biggest questions they wrestled with were "What was best for her dad? Did he want to continue to live on his own as much as possible or would he prefer to be with family?"

The next day after leaving her office, Hannah drove to her dad's house and talked with him. She laid out the options as they understood the situation and asked him what he saw as the best solution. Without hesitation, he told her that if possible, he wanted to be with family. He was concerned, however, about the extra burden it would be for them. He did not want to interfere with their own lives and keep them from doing what they wanted to do.

Hannah assured him that it would be a privilege for them to have him in their home. It would mean strengthening the family bond and giving the children a chance to experience a relationship with their grandfather that many other children would never have. She told her dad that having him in their home would only make their lives that much richer.

A few weeks later, her dad had assigned the house to a Realtor and moved into a room with his daughter and her family. From the first day, it was a pleasant experience. There were no regrets, no hard feelings, and no second thoughts.

With Hannah's dad in their home, their children could spend time with their grandfather, learn from him what it was like when he grew up, ask his help with homework, and do things with him on a daily basis. This experience also taught them all that older people can contribute much, if only they were not ignored. This example of not "living for me" but living for others shows how great the rewards can be and how much people miss if they live for themselves.

Neither couple did anything that could be judged as wrong. Each made a decision according to their present situation and in line with their motives. In the matter of elder care, there is no answer that fits every situation, but when a decision is made based entirely, or mostly, for selfish reasons, then it is an unbiblical and unwise decision. The ones who make such decisions end up losing out on so many wonderful experiences.

Living for others can give the giver so much by way of rewards. There is the freedom of knowing you did the right thing, and there is the joy of knowing that someone else benefited from your decision and action. You may become richer in relationships or in experiences for having someone else's welfare in mind, rather than your own pleasure.

Pause and Reflect

What is your relationship with your parents or grandparents like?

Would you squeeze them into your home if they were unable to live on their own? Why or why not?

What kinds of circumstances would prevent you from having a senior family member live with you?

The Bible tells us that anyone who neglects the needs of his family is worse than an unbeliever in his motives and actions. Does that apply to our modern culture where skilled and trained people are willing to take on the responsibility for their care?

If you are forced by circumstances to place elderly family members in professional care, what can you do to maintain a strong family bond?

Do you know anyone who has regretted placing a family member is such care? Why do you think it bothers them?

For those people you know who have kept elderly family members in their home, did it work well or was it a challenge for them? Does their experience influence your own decision in this matter?

In Conclusion

The strangest things happen when we learn to live with others in mind. Over time, through hardships and trials, by failures and disappointments, and by standing firm to our commitments, we grow closer to each other, and each of us finds that our own desires have changed such that we are fulfilled by this blessed relationship based on mutual giving rather than on selfish taking. When we come to a place where we realize that, we can give God thanks.

Not everything shown by these examples will accurately reflect the situation you may be in. Every couple, every family, and every challenge has its own unique elements. But the basic concept is still true. You may not have the close caring relationship of Mark and Hannah, but you can still learn to see things from the perspective of someone else. The key is being open to new ways of doing things before and in the many stages of your marriage. Since we are all basically selfish, it may take a very long time to move from where you are to where you want to be. You should always keep in mind the words of James (4:1–3), where he instructs us that every argument, every matter of discord, and every disagreement is rooted in selfishness. We want things the way we want them. We desire to have our own way. We argue and fight if we don't take the time to see things from another's perspective. He goes so far as to say that even the things we ask of God are sometimes requested with selfish motives.

With perseverance and a strong reliance on the Holy Spirit's help, you can move closer to the goal of having a long and happy marriage that is characterized by unselfish motives and actions rather than looking out for *me*. I can assure you that once you make that change, you and your spouse will certainly experience an amazing marriage.

Appendix

Thoughts on the Same Topics
Written in Verse for the
Poetically Minded Reader

I Believe in Marriage

You may think I am a slave to the whims of my wife
Because I lost my freedom, you say, trading it in for a chain.
But I wouldn't change a thing about my life.
If I had to, I would do it all over again.

You say I will probably be disappointed the way things go
Because life is never as easy as we would like it to be.
A fairy-tale ending is as rare as a Florida snow,
But that doesn't make it a nightmare, you see.

You talk like our marriage will not last for very long
Because you have seen so many others fall apart.
Statistics are often misleading and sometimes proven wrong
By those who do not listen but instead follow their heart.

You believe marriage is unnecessary, old-fashioned, or outdated
Because so many are ignoring the ceremony of love.
I'll answer that one is never really committed or truly mated
Unless one has pledged oneself before others and before God.

I believe marriage to be the most sacred union of two souls.
I believe a marriage can last through
times of trial, sickness, and pain.
I believe the journey of a good marriage
is better than any story told.
I believe there are no chains on love; we
gladly give and receive back again.

I refuse to listen to all the lies and the false ideas.
Rather, I will accept as truth that God knows what is best.
A marriage made in heaven will shatter all the fears
And last as long as life itself, passing every kind of test.

"No" Because

I am flattered that you asked me,
But the answer is, as far as I can see,
"No" because I'm busy with my business
and building my career.
"No" because I just bought a new home;
I want to settle here.
"No" because my family all live nearby.
You may want me to move.
"No" because I'm used to being alone,
not making meals for two.
"No" because I want to find pleasure
in the things I do myself.
"No" because (though this may break your heart)
I am in love with someone else.
So though I think you're wonderful and sweet,
I cannot marry you. But thanks for asking me.

Surely the One

When he asked to meet me, it was in a public place.
I had no good reason to say no and stay away.
We chatted and laughed freely among some of his friends.
Right away, we both knew how it was going to end.
He was not the one for me.

I dated several more men to see if I could find
Someone I could give my love and expect his in kind.
After a few bad times of hurt, pain, and rejection,
I met a man who was kind, loving, and respectful.
He was surely the one God meant for me.

When she agreed to go with me to hike mountain trails,
I didn't know she was afraid of spiders, snakes, and snails.
Because she held such deep-felt fear and didn't trust my care,
It wasn't long before it was clear we were not a pair.
She was not the one for me.

After trying to win one girl after another,
I decided there was no one just like my mother.
About to quit with no more hope, as far as I could see,
I met a woman who fulfilled all of my human dreams.
She was surely the one God meant for me.

Why Marry?

Marion caught my eye and later my heart.
As our relationship grew, we became very close.
Romance is great; it's a wonderful feeling.
Reality should be as exciting as this.
I knew I could love her right from the start,
And she had similar feelings, I suppose.
Good things have come from that first meeting.
Every day we're living in a state of bliss.

I knew the bubble had to one day burst,
So it was no surprise when trouble began;

Nothing major, but a difficulty no less.
One that together we were able to survive.
The question was "Which bill should we pay first:

Five hundred for the rent or three for the gas?"
Our small income didn't meet all our debt.
Receiving welfare was what saved our lives.

Marriage has never been seriously considered by us.
Everyone says it would only make the situation worse.

The Question

Each night seemed to bring its own excitement.
After working a full shift, it was a welcome pace.
She knew that if her lover didn't come over,
At least he would call to say how much he cared.
One weekend they had been together and spent
All their time visiting friends in another state.
She felt a little like she was a display trophy,
Yet her pride in him showed in the joys they shared.

They got to know each other rather fast.
Much time was spent doing things they both liked
And in long discussions about family, life, and careers.
After several weeks, they both knew what they wanted.
Theirs was a commitment that would last.
She knew that there would be an occasional fight
And not everything would happen without a few tears,
But in spite of that, their love was undaunted.

He was coming over this evening
To take her out to dinner and a dance.
They hadn't been out for several days,
And she really needed him to give her some cheer.
When he came, his face was beaming.
She knew from that to expect a night of romance.
What she did not expect—not that night anyway—
Was the *question* that every woman wants to hear.

Her response was quick and sure.
"Oh yes! Oh darling! Of course!
A thousand times yes! It's so beautiful!"
The ring had fit her finger so well.
The rest of the evening was a blur.
She said, "I love you," until she was hoarse,
And he answered with "You're so wonderful."
Neither wanted to be the first to break the spell.

Waiting

Will you be mine and mine alone to cherish and obey?
I'll stand by you forever, not just for a season, a month, or a day.
Will you solemnly pledge to love and help me as long as life shall last,
Though the trials we will face together are many?

Where has your beloved gone? When will he be back?
How long will you wait?
The questions seemed so frequent, so personal, so fast.
I didn't know all the answers they were trying to find so I put them off,
hoping to find peace and assurance in my own mind.

Sometimes the waiting seems endless and mundane.
Your absence wears on me.
Sometimes I wonder just how much longer I can wait.
I know I promised to be faithful, loyal, and true, but the temptations are strong
for me to give up, walk away, and forget all about you.

I heard from my betrothed, my beloved, my friend when he sent a message
to say he was coming home and the waiting would end.
Soon he would be here to take me to his home after the wedding day.
Then I will be his, and he will be mine alone.

My Wedding Banquet

I'm sitting at the table spread for me.
I'm feasting on the harvest of the fields.
No words can ever express the way I feel
As I behold the bounty as far as I can see.

I'm not a guest at this wedding feast today.
At the head table I get to preside
With my groom so regally at my side.
We celebrate our joyous marriage in this grand way.

There are people present that my husband asked
Whom I would never think to invite,
But what a wonderful, beautiful sight
To see a crowd so diverse, so happy, so vast.

I turn toward my groom and look into his eyes
And see triumph, joy, and pleasure.
This moment I will always treasure
In the years ahead as we live forever side by side.

The Answer Would Still Be "I Do"

Our love was born one day so many years ago.
God brought us together, your sweet soul and mine.
Hand in hand we started, not knowing where we'd go
But certain that our love would keep us for all time.
I belong by your side.
I belong here with you.
Darling, if today you'd ask me,
The answer would still be "I do."

We stood by each other in good times and bad;
In sickness and in health our love was there to stay.
Though sometimes I may fail, make you upset or mad,
I want you to know that there's just one thing to say:
I belong by your side.
I belong here with you.
Darling, if today you'd ask me,
The answer would still be "I do."

We can't know the future and all that lies ahead,
But this one thing you know: my love for you is strong.
I'll stand by you, sweetheart, 'til I take my last breath.
If you've ever wondered where my heart and soul belong,
I belong by your side.
I belong here with you.
Darling, if today you'd ask me,
The answer would still be "I do."

Self-Reflection[1]

She looked at herself in the washroom mirror and wondered if it was worth all the effort.

This job seemed like a good idea at the time, but now the rhythm, the drudgery, the dullness have set in.

It's true that financially they were freer than they had ever been before.

Her income added to what they could provide for their children, their home, and their friends.

The ad she had answered seemed rather appealing.

"No experience necessary," it said. "We'll train."

So she hired on to bake bread for a living.

Now, eighteen months later, she wondered why.

Every morning her family missed her leaving, and often in the evening, it was the same: never home, never available, not there giving hugs, kisses, or encouragement; always saying goodbye.

She often made excuses not to go to events at school or in the community.

She was either too busy or too tired to go.

Exhaustion was her constant companion these days.

The children, begging and pleading, had begun to resent her being gone so completely.

It was like they had no mother at all.

Her husband also had more than a few complaints.

Her break being over, she returned to her work, but her heart was no longer in it.

She had come to realize she had traded away family closeness and love for a weekly paycheck.

The rest of the day she kept watch on the clock.

She couldn't wait for the day to end.

In her mind, she rehearsed what she would say to her family and wondered how they would react.

She waited until after dinner to share the news with the children, her husband giving his consent.

---

[1] © Ken Hinkley. *From the Journey of a Heart.* Trafford Publishing, 2003.

They started asking questions all at once, knowing this would affect their lives greatly.

Seeing the positive reactions, she really knew the decision to stay home was the best.

No job at any price could replace the hugs the love and the joys of being a family.

On Giving and Tithing

Another appeal came in the mail asking us to make a contribution.
We would love to help and study our budget to find a possible solution.
How much should we give? To whom should we send a donation check?
How do we set priority, determining who we should support and who we reject?
First of all, we know it must be a work of the Lord;
Those who minister in Jesus's name and help spread the word.
That means our local church and those it sends,
But how much on this one cause should we spend?
Some teach a tithe as if it were a law that we dare not break.
Others say we must give cheerfully to show how much we appreciate
All God is and does for us, knowing we could never repay
The acts of mercy, grace, and love he performs every day.
In real life terms, we are taught that our responsibilities insist
On a set of priorities that force us the temptations to resist
And focus on the necessities; the basic needs of living.
That is more important than deciding the where and how much of giving.
To give away what God has given for our daily bread
Is to violate the principles of God's word; what Jesus said.
To be an unreliable steward of what God has put into our care
May bring more troubles, more arguments, and lead to despair.
Here's the bottom line, the way to know what to do with funds:
Work to earn your living; that is always number one.
Meet basic family needs: shelter, clothes, transportation, and food.
Then as God richly blesses, share with others the bounty he has given you.
Your local church is a good place to start, this we are told.
Begin in your own community among the folks you know.
Those appeals that come so frequently in the mail should never replace
The help you offer those you can pray with and meet face-to-face.

Where to Live?

They had discussed many things as they looked ahead to their wedding day.

In their relationship, they had had to face many decisions relating to a life that would be shared.

They both had careers and job responsibilities that offered personal fulfillment as well as possible advancement.

What were they to do if and when those career opportunities created the need for displacement?

Now that they were going to be one family, whose career would control where they lived?

What about other factors, such as family connections, community ties, and other things?

If he wanted to live in the old homestead where Grandpa and Grandma raised their kids,

And she would prefer to live in another town closer to her work, whose way should win?

If she enjoyed volunteering at the Y, singing in a choir, and had close friends nearby,

Should she move some distance away and lose all that to please him and his boss?

Where should we live after the wedding? Should we stay close by or go to another community?

The decision is not always an easy one but one that should lead to unity, peace, love, and tranquility.

The Child

He had noticed that a change had come over her.
She seemed to be subject to whims.
Often when they were at home together, she would act silly.
Or for no reason at all, she would break down and cry.
She had no explanation for what occurred,
At least that's what she told him.
But the truth was that her body was changing quickly.
There was the possibility of another life deep down inside.
It occurred to her that it had been too many days
Since she recalled her last cyclical interruption.
Could it be? Is it possible? What does this mean?
To ease her mind, she bought a home test kit.
After her shopping was done and she was on her way,
The anxiety that drove her home soon changed to anticipation.
"This is me! Oh, I hope it's true. My man will be so pleased."
By the time she arrived, she knew she wanted this.
His reaction to the test results was typically male.
He was excited. He was glad. He was proud.
There would have to be some changes made around the place,
Beginning with the unused room in the back.
In the end, her judgment and good sense prevailed.
Soft toys and baby things were allowed
But not the bike, the mitt, or the roller skates;
Not even the train with miles of track.
The news has spread to all their family and friends.
The pages on the calendar flew quickly by.
She took a leave of absence for about a year
To learn the art of motherhood as well as she could.
One day in the spring, the waiting came to an end.
With her doctor's help and her husband by her side,
Their child arrived amid the pain, the sweat, and the tears.
They were a family now, and it felt good.

One Last Round of Golf

As he threw his golf clubs into the back of his SUV,
His spirit lifted as he looked forward to the first tee.
The weather was nice, and the winds were calm.
The sun as it rose promised to be warm.
What a good time he would have to enjoy and relax
Until his round was over and he had to get back.

But getting back was not what he really wanted to do,
Because he knew that his wife would continue the feud
That had erupted when he had told her his plans.
He just has to golf whenever he can.
After a week of working long, hard days,
He needed to unwind, to just get far away.

When he was not golfing, he found other means
To occupy his time or to blow off steam.
Staying at home didn't even cross his mind.
He thought his wife was quite cruel and unkind
To insist that he spend his weekend at home.
Sometimes he wished that he would find them gone.

Arriving home, he found a note to say that she was sorry
But told him that he did not need to worry.
That she and the kids were fine with her mom.
If he didn't need them, as he had often said,
Then they didn't need him to be warm and fed.

He pleaded with her to change her stubborn mind.

He promised that he would be more attentive and kind.
He had not understood how much she really meant to him
Or how much he was missed by all three of his kids.
Could she come back by the end of the day?
One last round of golf is all he wanted to play.
Her answer was as sure as the day was long.
It was either golf or learn to live alone.

Suspicions and Doubt[2]

Yesterday she had found a note in his dirty shirt. There was no mistake in what he wrote. The words were clear. "Love you" is simple and direct. But who was Jenny? Thank God for this unfaithful man? She didn't think so. Last night they had shouted and screamed about the matter. He said it wasn't what it seemed to be at all. She wanted to believe him in her heart, but how could she? This other woman was pulling them apart, and it hurt. Deciding she would stick it out until they had another talk, she reluctantly answered the shrill ring of the telephone. "Hello, this is Jenny," said a lovely voice. Her anger flared. "I'm calling to see if you were home. I have a delivery." When she put the phone down, her hand was shaking. Her anger and jealousy were all gone, replaced by embarrassment. The man she had so quickly despised had taken it all away by ordering a special gift as a surprise to show her his love. The tears flowed out of embarrassment, shame, and humility. What a fool she had been not to trust him.

After so many years together, she should have known he would never shame or hurt her in any way. The note she had found in his pocket had been a reminder to himself not to forget what he wanted to buy. Jenny ran a flower and gift shop specializing in custom orders. Her favorite flower was certainly not a common variety. He had gone out of his way to please her. Hanging from the large bouquet was a card. "I love you" was written in red. Three simple words. "Thank you, Lord" was all she said.

---

[2] Excerpted from "Confrontation" by the author, May 1998.

Mark and Mike

Mark

He saw the magazine lying on the floor of the boys' high school locker room.
Out of curiosity, he picked it up, then threw it down in disgust.
The pictures he saw made him feel ashamed.
He pledged he would never look at that again.
However, the images were planted deep in his mind where only he could see.
When he was alone, though he said he wouldn't, he went online to sites where he shouldn't.
Before he knew what was going on, it was what he thought about all the time.
His grades slipped to an all-time low; he spent more and more time alone.
His family finally found out his addiction and gave him some very severe restrictions.
But the lust that was born down in his soul would not be erased, not lose its control.
In the end, though he denied it was true, his addiction cost him all that was good.

Mike

A friend gave him the paperback book.
After reading a few pages, he knew he was hooked.
The more he read, the more he wanted to read.
There was no real harm that he could see.
It was only fiction, after all; no real people were actually involved.
He reasoned to himself that all was fine.
There was no lasting effect on his young mind.
But the images and events described played themselves out as if alive.
There didn't seem to be an escape from the filth he had read on every page.

He bowed his head and confessed his shame, begged forgiveness in Jesus's name, and vowed to never let that kind of vice intentionally become a part of his life.

With the help of God's Holy Spirit, he would shun that habit and never do it.

By perseverance, prayer, and helpful friends, he never gave in to that temptation again.

A Father's Advice

"My dear wife," declared the husband as they gazed upon the newborn child, "you have presented me with a son for which I am immensely proud."

"And to you, my son," he said as he lifted the baby in his arms, "I must say that I will do all I can to protect you from harm.

"I am humbled to think that God Almighty would give me the privilege and the great responsibility of rearing you.

"As I look into your beautiful face, so innocent, so carefree, so content, so mild,

"I must warn you that I am new at this and every piece of advice I give you may not be sound.

"But as we learn together, as I learn to lead and you learn to follow, you needn't be alarmed. Every decision that we make in life helps define who we are, whether a wise man or a fool. You, my son, will learn to live with dignity, not shame, and proudly help carry on the family name."

"Have you noticed," he asked his wife, "how much our son has grown? What a joy he brings! You have nurtured him well and have coddled him these last few years.

"But now, I'm afraid, he must venture out into society and learn to make friends. He must learn to interact with others his age, as we prepare him to enter school."

He called to him the boy who came with arms outstretched, pretending he had wings.

Running too fast, he tripped and fell. Father was there quickly to wipe away the tears.

"You know, my son," he gently chided, "if you don't be careful, that's often how it ends. Every decision that we make in life helps define who we are, whether a wise man or a fool. You, my son, will learn to live with dignity, not shame, and proudly help carry on the family name."

"Our son," he told his wife, "is coming soon to manhood. Look how tall he stands! You should be as proud as I am of his strength, his character, and his skills.

"Yet there is much work to be done. In these last few years, our parenting will be put to the test.

"Let's pray that God, who gave him to us, will give us wisdom to see him through."

As they sat together, they faced their son with anxiety in their hearts and trembling hands.

"Son," said the father, "I know the temptations to try new things are great, but there are many that kill. You must learn to take a stand to avoid such things, even if you're not like the rest.

"Every decision that we make in life helps define who we are, whether a wise man or a fool. You, my son, will learn to live with dignity, not shame, and proudly help carry on the family name."

"My dear wife," declared the husband as they looked at their newlywed child,

"We have raised ourselves an upright, God-fearing man, of whom we both should be glad." "To our son," he began the toast, then he couldn't help but brag, every word of which he meant sincerely. And at the end, all he could say, amid the tears, was "We are proud of you."

As they sat at the festive table, many folks they did not know greeted them with endless smiles.

He thought back to the time, a few months ago, when things for his son looked really, really bad.

His son had come to him to seek his fatherly advice, which he offered freely.

"Every decision that we make in life helps define who we are, whether a wise man or a fool. You, my son, will learn to live with dignity, not shame, and proudly help carry on the family name."

Family Vacation

The car was finally packed. She and the children made endless trips. Back and forth they went like ants stuffing in everything that could fit. Sleeping bags and fishing rods; pots, pans, basic foods, and rain gear; clothes, a lantern, games, sports balls; first aid kit, tackle box, swimwear. They were ready to go.

The miles steadily whizzed by. Two of the kids had fallen asleep after the excitement died. The third played a game that buzzed and beeped. Two hours later, another scene; the peace she had enjoyed so much gave way to whimpers and screams. The baby was wet. Time for lunch. They were ready to stop.

They were under way again, but now the magic had been broken. The children wouldn't behave, and her husband had hardly spoken. She suggested something to do to keep them occupied, refereed a fight or two, and the baby started to cry. Their spirits were drooping.

Evening was coming soon. Only a few more miles left today. Their motel, the Silver Moon, would let them stretch their legs, romp, and play. It would be good to get out. Something besides sitting to do would be a relief, no doubt. When the motel came into view, their spirits soon picked up.

The second day was better. They got under way by eight o'clock. Everyone's mood was brighter, looking forward to the final stop. They should arrive after noon. Then they could set the children free. Watching carefully, they soon saw their cabin among the trees in a beautiful spot.

She took in the pleasant sight. Her children were in the water, splashing with all of their might. Sometimes they would yell loudly for her. Her husband was tending the grill, cooking up some delicious food. She wanted time to stand still; shouldn't life always be this good? What a beautiful thought.

The week quickly disappeared. All too soon, they were on their way in spite of protest and tears. Too soon their time together was gone. Too soon they retraced their route back to another place and time. Too soon they found the old groove with schedules and the daily grind. Vacation was over.

Do I Get a Volunteer?

I see needs and opportunities all around us. Where do I begin?
I could coach a team or drive a bus, bake cookies, cakes, and pies, but what can I do best?
My children need a carpool driver, chaperone at a dance, and someone to make the event flyers, pass out invitations, or just be there for counsel and advice.
I could choose one or more of these many opportunities, or I could go my own way and not listen to all the clamoring voices.
I must decide each time I'm asked if this is what I should be doing and is it good for my family?
It would be so easy to give all my time to help others with their projects, but God gave me this family of mine to hold, to teach to cherish, and I can't do that if I'm too busy or gone.
Do I get a volunteer? I hear the imploring words again.
I do not raise my hand.
Instead I say, "Good luck," to my hardworking friends. "I wish you well and much success, but I'm volunteering my time at home."

What Do We Do with Mom?

"Mom, are you all right?" A panicked voice was on the phone.
"You know how much we worry with you living alone."
"It's okay, dear," the mother answered sweetly. "There's nothing
wrong.
I just wanted to call since I haven't heard from you in so long."
"We talked only yesterday," the son replied. "Do you not recall?
I thought you had had a spell or maybe taken a fall."
"Oh, dear, I didn't mean to upset you," she replied,
"But maybe you could come visit me sometime."
"I'll do that. I promise I will be there tomorrow," he said.
As he hung up, he wondered what was going on in her head.

He discussed the options with his wife who understood so well.
His mom should no longer be alone. That much they could tell.
But what choices do they have? To send her to a senior home
Would relieve their fears of her being left alone,
But would she want to live among strangers the rest of her days?
They hoped they could find a better place for her to stay.
In the end, after talking to the rest of the children,
They came to what they believed would be a workable solution.
Mom would come to live with them, their home to share
And enjoy the tenderness of her family's loving care.

Printed in the United States
By Bookmasters